Penguin Books
Yukio Mishima on Hagakure

Yukio Mishima was born in Tokyo in 1925. When he
graduated from the Peers' School in 1944, he received a
citation from the Emperor as the highest honour student.
In 1947 he graduated from the Tokyo Imperial University
School of Jurisprudence, and the following year published his
first novel. As a writer he was both prolific and highly
acclaimed: *The Sound of Waves* (*Shiosai*) won the 1954
Shinchosha Literary Prize and *The Temple of the Golden
Pavilion* received the Yomiuri Literary Prize for 1957. Though
best known for his novels, of which he wrote fifteen, he also
wrote more than fifty short stories, many plays – notably five
modern Nō dramas – several volumes of essays and a travel
book. Among his books published in English are *The Lady Aoi*,
The Sailor Who Fell from Grace with the Sea, *Forbidden
Colours*, *Thirst for Love*, *Spring Snow*, *Runaway Horses*, *Temple
of Dawn* and *The Decay of the Angel*, all of which have been
published in Penguins.

Immediately after the Second World War, Yukio Mishima
went to the United States as a guest of the State Department
and of *Partisan Review*. As his interests were not those of a
passive intellectual, he acted in many films, directed his own
film, *Yokoku*, and was a serious devotee of weight-lifting and
body-building.

Mishima firmly upheld the traditions of Japan's imperial
past, which he believed were being swiftly eroded by Western
materialism. Not only by his life – which, much influenced by
the Samurai ethic, carefully followed his philosophy of action
– but by his death as well, Yukio Mishima hoped to return
his country to the values of its past. In 1970 he astounded the
world when he and a colleague committed ritual suicide,
hara-kiri, by disembowelment.

Yukio Mishima on Hagakure

The Samurai Ethic and Modern Japan

Penguin Books

Penguin Books Ltd, Harmondsworth,
Middlesex, England
Penguin Books, 625 Madison Avenue,
New York, New York 10022, U.S.A.
Penguin Books Australia Ltd, Ringwood,
Victoria, Australia
Penguin Books Canada Ltd, 2801 John Street,
Markham, Ontario, Canada L3R 1B4
Penguin Books (N.Z.) Ltd, 182–190 Wairau Road,
Auckland 10, New Zealand

Hagakure Nyuman (Introduction to Hagakure) by Yukio Mishima
first published in the USA 1977
Published in Great Britain by Souvenir Press 1977
Published in Penguin Books 1979

This book is published by arrangement through Orion
    Press Tokyo and Souvenir Press Ltd

Set, printed and bound in Great Britain by
Cox & Wyman Ltd, Reading
Set in Linotype Times

Contents

Contents

The Forty-eight Vital Principles
of *Hagakure*

How to Read *Hagakure*

Appendix

Translator's Note

In August 1967, three years before his dramatic ritual suicide at the Self Defense Force Headquarters in Tokyo, Yukio Mishima wrote this fascinating book – his personal interpretation of the classic samurai ethics and behaviour, *Hagakure* (literally, 'Hidden among the Leaves'). Immediately following Mishima's suicide in November 1970, it became an overwhelming bestseller in Japan. The many who admired him, as well as the others who despised his political positions, turned to *Hagakure* to help them understand Mishima's final drama.

The best known line in the original *Hagakure*, quoted by many who have never read the work itself, is: 'I have discovered that the Way of the Samurai is death.' The author continues: 'In a fifty-fifty life or death crisis, simply settle it by choosing immediate death. There is nothing complicated about it. Just brace yourself and proceed ... One who chooses to go on living having failed in one's mission will be despised as a coward and a bungler ... In order to be a perfect samurai, it is necessary to prepare oneself for death morning and evening, day in and day out.'

One of Mishima's many self-images was that of a modern day samurai. It was essential to him that he die while still in his prime and that his death be worthy of the samurai tradition. Even details of the staging of the scene of his death at the Self Defense Force Headquarters show *Hagakure* influence: The sweatbands worn by Mishima and his companions as he delivered his final, passionate address bore a

Hagakure slogan. And his particularly fastidious attention to grooming on the morning of his last day reflects the spirit of *Hagakure* as Mishima understood it. 'Men must be the colour of cherry blossoms, even in death.'

The original *Hagakure* contains the teachings of the samurai-turned-priest Jōchō Yamamoto (1659–1719), written down and edited by his student Tsuramoto Tashiro. For generations the manuscript was preserved as moral and practical instruction for the daimyo and samurai retainers in the Nabeshima House of Saga Han in Northern Kyushu. For about one hundred and fifty years, until the Meiji Restoration of 1868, however, *Hagakure* was apparently guarded as secret teachings shown only to a chosen few. The Nabeshima House presumably wanted to keep such valuable, practical instruction to itself. (It is also possible that the intense loyalty to the Nabeshima daimyo advocated in *Hagakure* might have seemed subversive to the central military government had the manuscript been circulated.)

Hagakure became available to the reading public for the first time in the Meiji Era, when its principles of loyalty were re-interpreted in terms of loyalty to the emperor and the Japanese nation. In the nationalistic fervour of the 1930s, several editions and commentaries were published, lavishly extolling Jōchō's teachings as *yamato-damaschii*, 'the unique spirit of the Japanese'. During the Second World War, editions proliferated and sold in staggering numbers. 'I found that the Way of the Samurai is death,' became a slogan used to spur young Kamikaze pilots to their death. After the war, *Hagakure* was quickly abandoned as dangerous and subversive. Many copies were destroyed so they would not meet the eyes of the Occupation authorities.

Of course, *Hagakure* is not merely a book about death. The original is an enormous compilation including moral and practical instruction for samurai, as well as information on local history and the exploits of specific warriors. Mishima deals only with the first three volumes and emphasizes, in addition to death (but not unrelated, of course), action, subjectivity, strength of character, passion, and love (in most cases homosexual love). He also delights in showing us prolific examples of Jōchō's practical advice for daily living: from suggestions on how to hold a meeting, proper behaviour at a drinking party, to child rearing, and suppressing a yawn in public. Mishima draws parallels between the moral decay of Jōchō's day and that of postwar Japan, explaining how Jōchō's advice has helped him live an anachronistic and therefore worthwhile life.

Mishima stresses the significant role *Hagakure* played in his development during the war and after, and discusses similarities between his own criticisms of materialistic postwar Japan and Jōchō's criticisms of the sumptuous decadence of his contemporaries. Mishima seems quite close to Jōchō in his ideas of personal morality. In their insistence on the spiritual and physical perfection of the self, both men seem to be basically asocial; both are concerned with personal motivation, with *how* one performs rather than to what effect. Always the emphasis is on the individual, whose ultimate goal is self-cultivation rather than contribution to his immediate environment or to society.

Mishima's twist or genius was to apply to modern society the severest social criticism of the samurai ethic found in *Hagakure*. His fiction often deals with the atomization of modern society and the impossibility of spiritual or emotional communication between people. But in Mishima's later works, entwined with the despair of individual isolation, is the exultation of self-sufficiency. Everything that interests a Mishima hero he can do by himself. He needs no one, nor does he care what anyone else needs. Such an attitude found ultimate fulfilment in Mishima's death for the sake of an emperor who had no interest in him, for a cause to which he knew he would contribute nothing – and by his own hand. The way towards that violent, yet fascinating death may be found in the pages that follow.

KATHRYN SPARLING
Columbia University
January 1977

Prologue

Hagakure and I

Raymond Radiguet's *Le Bal du Comte d'Orgel* and *The Collected Works of Akinari Ueda*

The spiritual companions of youth are friends and books. Friends have flesh-and-blood bodies and are constantly changing. Enthusiasms at one stage in one's life cool with the passage of time, giving way to different enthusiasms shared with a different friend. In a sense, this is true of books, too. Certainly there are times when a book that has inspired us in our childhood, picked up and reread years later, loses its vivid appeal and seems a mere corpse of the book we remember. But the biggest difference between friends and books is that whereas friends change, books do not. Even gathering dust neglected in a corner of some case, a book doggedly preserves its character and its philosophy. By accepting or rejecting it, reading it or not, we can change the book through our attitude towards it, but that is all.

My childhood was spent during the war. In those days the book that thrilled me most was a novel by Raymond Radiguet, *La Bal du Comte d'Orgel*. It is a masterpiece of classical technique that has ranked Radiguet with the great masters of French literature. The artistic value of his works is beyond question, but admittedly at that time my appreciation of them was half for the wrong reasons. I was drawn to the genius Radiguet, who at the tender age of twenty had died leaving the world such a masterpiece, and I who was almost certainly destined to go to war and die equally young in battle superimposed my own image on his. Somehow he became my personal rival and his literary achievements a landmark to be reached before I died. Consequently, as my literary tastes changed and I unexpectedly survived on into the postwar era, the spell of Radiguet's novel naturally weakened.

The other book is *The Collected Works of Akinari Ueda* (scholar, poet, and novelist of the late Edo Period), which I carried around with me during the air raids.[1] Why at that stage I was so devoted to Akinari Ueda I still do not really know. Quite possibly I had come to nurture within me as my ideal image of Japanese fiction Akinari's conscious anachronism and the exquisite artistry of his short stories, which seemed to me like burnished jewels. My respect for Akinari and for Radiguet has not lessened to this day, but gradually these two ceased to be my constant companions.

The One and Only Book for Me, *Hagakure*

There is one more book, and that is Jōchō Yamamoto's *Hagakure*. I began reading it during the war, when I kept it always on or near my desk, and if there is one single book I have referred to continually in the twenty years since, rereading a passage now and then according to the occasion, never failing to be moved anew, that book is *Hagakure*. In particular, it was after the extraordinary popularity of *Hagakure*, after its wartime pre-eminence as socially obligatory reading had ended, that its light began to shine within me. Maybe *Hagakure* is after all fundamentally a book destined to paradox. During the war, *Hagakure* was like a luminescent object in broad daylight, but it is in pitch darkness that *Hagakure* radiates its true light.

Shortly after the war, I made my debut as a novelist. At that time there swirled around me the new literary currents of a new era. But the era of what is called postwar literature[2] created no resonance within me, either intellectually or as a writer. The vitality and energy of people with intellectual and philosophical roots different from mine, with literary sensibilities alien to me, rushed past me like a storm; that was all. Of course, I felt the loneliness of my position. And I asked myself what it was that had served consistently as my ultimate guiding principle during the war years and would continue to do so now that the war was over. It was not Marx's dialectical materialism, nor was it the Imperial Rescript on Education. The book that was to provide constant spiritual guidance must form the basis of my morality and it must enable me to approve completely of my youth. It must be a book that could support firmly this loneliness of mine and my anachronistic stance. What is more, it must be a book banned by contemporary society. *Hagakure* conformed to all these specifications. This book, like all others made much of during the war, came to be thought of as a loathsome, ugly, evil book, a tainted book to be wiped from memory, tied roughly in bundles, and consigned to the rubbish heap. Thus, in the darkness of our age, *Hagakure* for the first time radiates its true light.

Hagakure, the Book That Teaches Freedom and Passion

It was now that what I had recognized during the war in *Hagakure* began to manifest its true meaning. Here was a book that preached freedom, that taught passion. Those who have read carefully only the most famous line from *Hagakure* still retain an image of it as a book of odious fanaticism. In that one line, 'I found that the Way of the Samurai is death,' may be seen the paradox that symbolizes the book as a whole. It was this sentence, however, that gave me the strength to live.

My Testimony

I first confessed my devotion to *Hagakure* after the war, in an article published in 1955 called 'Writer's Holiday'. The statement was as follows:

I began reading *Hagakure* during the war, and even now I read it from time to time. It is a strange book of peerless morality; its irony is not the deliberate irony of a cynic but irony that arises naturally from the discrepancy between knowledge of proper conduct and decision to act. What an energetic, soul-refreshing, what a human book.

Those who read *Hagakure* from the point of view of established convention, feudal morality for instance, are almost totally insensitive to its exhilaration. This book is brimming with the exuberance and freedom of people who lived under the restrictions of a rigid social morality. This morality lived in the very fabric of the society and its economic system. It was the one premise to their existence, and under this premise all was a glorification of energy and passion. Energy is good; lethargy is evil. An astonishing understanding of the world is unfolded in *Hagakure* without the slightest tinge of cynicism. Its effect is the direct opposite of the unpleasant aftertaste of La Rochefoucauld, for instance.

One rarely finds a book that liberates self-respect in ethical terms as much as does *Hagakure*. It is impossible to value energy while rejecting self-respect. Here there can be no such thing as going too far. Even arrogance is ethical (*Hagakure* does not, however, deal with arrogance in the abstract). 'A samurai must have confidence that he is the best and bravest warrior in all Japan.' 'A samurai must take great pride in his military valour; he must have the supreme resolution to die a fanatic's death.' There is no such thing as correctness or propriety in fanaticism.

The practical ethics for daily living taught by *Hagakure* might be called a man of action's belief in expediency. On fashion, Jōchō remarks nonchalantly, 'Thus it is essential to do things properly in every age.' Expediency is nothing more than an ethically fastidious rejection of extreme refinement of any kind. One must be stubborn, and eccentric. From ancient times most samurai have been of eccentric spirit, strong willed, and courageous.

Just as all artistic creations are born of a resistance to one's era, these teachings of Jōchō Yamamoto were recorded against a background of the extravagant, luxurious tastes of the Genroku and Hōei Eras [1688–1704; 1704–9] . . .

'I Found That the Way of the Samurai Is Death'

When Jōchō says, 'I found that the Way of the Samurai is death,' he is expressing his Utopianism, his principles of freedom and happiness. That is why we are able to read *Hagakure* today as the tale of an ideal country. I am almost certain that if such an ideal land were ever to materialize, its inhabitants would be far happier and freer than we are today. But what actually existed is merely Jōchō's dream.

The author of *Hagakure* devised a cure too potent for the modern malady. Presaging a splintering of the human spirit, he warned of the unhappiness of such a division, 'It is wrong to set one's mind on two things at once.' We must resurrect a faith in purity and its glorification. Jōchō, who could not help recognizing the validity of any kind of passion as long as it was genuine, well understood passion's laws . . .

The Misfortune and the Happiness of the Man of Action

Whether to consider natural death, or as *Hagakure* does, death by the sword or disembowelment as the proper completion of a man's training to perfection, it seems to me makes little difference. The fact that one is expected to be a man of action does not alter or ease in any way the law that human beings must bear the passage of 'Time'. 'In a fifty-fifty life or death situation, simply settle it by choosing immediate death.' Jōchō is merely preaching the good common sense that whatever the situation, self-abandonment guarantees a minimum of virtue.

And a truly fifty-fifty situation does not come along often. It is significant that while Jōchō chooses to emphasize the decision to die quickly, he obscures the criteria for judging when a situation is in fact 'fifty-fifty'. The evaluation that ultimately produces the decision to die trails behind it a long chain of evaluations and resultant decisions to live, and this ceaseless tempering of one's judgement towards the final decision suggests the long period of tension and concentration that the man of action must endure. To the man of action, life frequently appears as a circle to be completed by the addition of one last point. From instant to instant he continues to discard such circles, incomplete because of one missing point, and goes on to be confronted by a succession of similar circles. In contrast, the life of an artist or philosopher appears as an accumulation of gradually widening concentric circles around himself. But when death finally arrives, who will have the greater sense of fulfilment, the man of action, or the artist? I should think that a death which in an instant completes one's world by the addition of a single point would afford a more intense feeling of fulfilment by far.

The greatest calamity for the man of action is that he fail to die even after that last unmistakable point has been added.

Yoichi Nasu lived long after he shot his arrow neatly through the fan held up for a target.[3] Jōchō's teachings on death emphasize the true happiness of the man of action rather than the external fact of the action itself. And Jōchō, who dreamed of attaining this happiness, wanted to commit suicide at the age of forty-two on the death of his lord, Mitsushige Nabeshima (second generation daimyo of the Nabeshima house), but was prevented from doing so by an interdiction against suicide in loyalty to the daimyo. Jōchō shaved his head, took Buddhist vows, and died a natural death at the age of sixty-one, reluctantly leaving *Hagakure* to posterity.

Hagakure, Womb of My Literary Oeuver

Even now, my thoughts on *Hagakure* have not changed much. Or rather, I suppose one could say that it was when I wrote this article that *Hagakure* first took shape within my consciousness, and I have devoted my passions and energy to living *Hagakure*, to practising *Hagakure* ever since. In short, I have come to be more and more deeply possessed by *Hagakure*. But I, who follow the way of the artist and entertainer condemned by *Hagakure*, have been tormented by the conflict between the action ethic and my art. The suspicion I had harboured for years, that there was inevitably something cowardly lurking beneath the surface of all literature, was articulated. In fact, to tell the truth, my firm insistence on the 'Combined Way of the Scholar and the Warrior'[4] I owe to the influence of *Hagakure*. Although I knew full well that there is no discipline so easy to speak of and so difficult to perform as the Combined Way of the Warrior and the Scholar, I decided that nothing else could offer me the excuse to live my life as an artist. This realization, too, I owe to *Hagakure*.

I am convinced, however, that art kept snugly within the bounds of art alone shrivels and dies, and in this sense I am no believer in what is commonly called art for art's sake. If art is not constantly threatened, stimulated by things outside its domain, it exhausts itself. Literary art takes its materials from life, but although life is thus the mother of literature, it is also her bitter enemy; although life is inherent in the author himself, it is also the eternal antithesis of art. All at once I recognized in *Hagakure* a philosophy of life, and somehow I felt that its beautiful, pristine world could stir up the quagmire that was the world of literature. For me, the meaning of *Hagakure* is in the vision of this pristine world, and although it is the influence of *Hagakure* that has made living as an artist so unusually difficult for me, at the same time *Hagakure* is the womb from which my writing is born. It is the eternal supplying source of my vitality – by its relentless whip, by its command, by its fierce criticism, because of its beauty, which is the beauty of ice.

Notes

1. Akinari Ueda (1734–1809). Scholar, poet, and writer of fiction of the late Edo Period, best known for his stylistically polished weird tales of the supernatural. His most famous work is probably *Ugetsu monogatari*, translated by Kengi Hamada as *Tales of Moonlight and Rain* (Columbia University Press, 1972). This work was the inspiration for the Kenji Mizoguchi movie *Ugetsu*.

2. Postwar literature refers specifically to novels and short stories written immediately after the war by a number of Leftist writers concerned with the war experience and the creation of a new postwar Japanese society.

3. Yoichi Nasu. A minor hero of the *Tales of the Heike* (early thirteenth-century war tales). Responding to a challenge, he is said to have shot an arrow through the centre of the rising sun painted on a fan attached to the gunwale of an enemy boat, though he was on horseback and despite wind and enormous distance.

4. The 'Combined Way of the Scholar and the Warrior'. The doctrine, emphasized by the Tokugawa government during its two hundred years of peace, that samurai should perfect themselves in literary or scholarly as well as military arts.

My *Hagakure*

Hagakure is Alive Today

The ultimate love I believe to be secret love. Once shared, love shrinks in stature. To pine away for love all one's years, to die of love without uttering the beloved's name, this is the true meaning of love. (Book Two)

Contemporary Youth Infatuated with the Cardin Look

During the twenty years immediately following the war, Japan began to transform herself into exactly the condition that *Hagakure* had foreseen. There were no longer any samurai in Japan, there was no war, the economy was reviving, all was overflowing with a mood of peace; youth was bored. *Hagakure*, to repeat, is basically a paradoxical book. When *Hagakure* says, 'The flower is red,' public opinion says, 'The flower is white.' When *Hagakure* says, 'One must not follow this course,' this course is exactly what the world at large is eagerly pursuing. Everything considered, behind that austere book *Hagakure* there lie social conditions and public opinions contrary to its contents. These conditions are the response that in any age the Japanese people have made to peacetime existence.

Here is one familiar example of this phenomenon. Certainly today is not the first time that men's fashions have flourished as though to outshine women's fashions. The sight of today's young men infatuated with the Cardin look is no novelty in Japanese history. In the Genroku Period

(Jōchō abandoned his worldly life to live in seclusion during the thirteenth year of Genroku, 1700), not only in clothing but extending even to the design of the swords they carried, their sword guards, and the dagger attached to the scabbard, a fashion for ornateness and dazzling splendour captivated the hearts of men. One look at the showy appurtenances and splendid pastimes depicted in the genre scrolls of Moronobu Hishikawa (*ukiyoe* artist of the early Edo Period) is enough to imagine the luxury of that age, influenced by the sumptuous culture of the merchants and townsmen.

Today, if you go to a jazz coffeehouse and speak with teenagers or young people in their twenties, you will find that they talk of absolutely nothing but how to dress smartly and cut a stylish figure. I once had the following experience. Having walked into a modern jazz café, I had no sooner seated myself at a table than a youth at the next table began to cross-examine me: 'Did you have those shoes made? Where did you have them made? And your cuff-links, where did you buy them? Where did you get the material for that suit? Who is your tailor?' He asked me one question after another in quick succession. Another youth, who was with the first, began giving him a hard time: 'Hey, cut it out. You sound like a beggar, asking questions like that. Why don't you just observe quietly and then steal his ideas?' And the first youth returned, 'Don't you think it's more honest to ask questions and learn from him openly?'

To learn, for them, meant to learn how to show themselves to their best advantage, to be initiated into the secrets of men's fashion. The following passage from *Hagakure* is clearly evidence of a similar attitude.

Times have changed in the last thirty years. When young samurai get together they talk of money, of profit and loss, how to run a household efficiently, how to judge the value of clothing, and they exchange stories about sex. If any other topic is mentioned, the atmosphere is spoiled and everyone present feels vaguely uncomfortable. What a distressing pass things have come to! (Book One)

The Feminization of the Male

Moreover, we are constantly being told of the feminization of Japanese males today – it is inevitably seen as the result of the influence of American democracy, 'ladies first', and so forth – but this phenomenon, too, is not unknown in our past. When, breaking away from the rough-and-tumble masculinity of a nation at war, the Tokugawa *bakufu* had securely established its hegemony as a peaceful régime, the feminization of Japanese males immediately began. One can see evidence of this trend in *ukiyo* prints of the eighteenth-century master Harunobu Suzuki: The couples snuggling together as they sit on the edge of the veranda gazing at plum blossoms so resemble each other in their hair styles, the cut and pattern of their clothes, the very expression on their faces that no matter how you examine them, no matter from what angle, it is impossible to tell which is the man and which is the woman. During the age in which *Hagakure* was written, this trend had already begun. Look at this scathing passage, called 'Female Pulse':

I heard this from an acquaintance of mine. Apparently a Doctor Kyōan once made the following statement: 'In medicine we distinguish between men and women by attributing to them the principles of yin and yang, and medical treatment originally differed accordingly. The pulse is also different. Over the past fifty years, however, the pulse of men has gradually become the same as that of women. Since noticing this phenomenon, I have considered it proper to treat eye diseases of male patients with the method normally appropriate to the pulse of women patients. When I try applying to my male patients the cures appropriate to men, they produce no effect whatever. The world is indeed entering a degenerate stage; men are losing their virility and are becoming just like women. This is an unshakeable truth I have learned from first-hand experience. I have decided to keep it a secret from the world at large.' When with this story in mind I look around me at the men of today, I often think to myself, 'Aha. There goes an example of a female pulse.' Almost never do I see what I call a true man ... (Book One)

Expense Account Aristocrats

The same thing can fairly be said of the rise of the expense account aristocrat, for which the modern tax system is at least partly responsible. In Jōchō's day the expense account samurai who had difficulty telling the difference between his own money and that of his lord had already become conspicuous. Within what was not a company but a daimyo domain, the young samurai, forgetting his objective of participating in the ideal of a cooperative community, had come to wish only for his own preservation. The idealistic gleam in the eyes of youth faded to a mere glimmer, and their attention was completely absorbed with trivialities. Young samurai with 'the furtive glance of pickpockets', who thought only of their own personal interest, had become increasingly numerous.

Looking at young samurai in service these days, it seems to me they set their sights pitifully low. They have the furtive glance of pickpockets. Most of them are out for their own interests, or to display their cleverness, and even those who seem calm of heart are simply putting up a good front. That attitude will never do. Unless a samurai sets his sights on no less than offering up his life for his ruler, dying swiftly and becoming a spirit, unless he is constantly anxious about the welfare of his daimyo and reports to him immediately whenever he has disposed of a problem, his concern being always to strengthen the foundations of the realm, he cannot be called a true samurai in the service of his lord. (Book One)

Lionized Baseball Players and Television Stars

While Jōchō condemns at great length people who distinguish themselves in a certain skill or art, he relates how his age is becoming imbued with a new tendency to idolize people who excel at such arts as the greatest stars of the day.

Today, baseball players and television stars are lionized. Those who specialize in skills that will fascinate an audience tend to abandon their existence as total human personalities and be reduced to a kind of skilled puppet. This tendency reflects the ideals of our time. On this point there is no difference between performers and technicians.

The present is the age of technocracy (under the leadership of technicians); differently expressed, it is the age of performing artists. One who excels at an art can win by means of that art the enthusiastic applause of society. At the same time, such people are lowering their life goals, aiming only at appearing as dashing and as important as possible. They forget the ideals for a total human being; to degenerate into a single cog, a single function, becomes their greatest ambition. In the light of this phenomenon, Jōchō's disdain for technicians and artists refreshes the soul:

That an art or skill will help one earn a living is true only of samurai from other domains. For samurai of this ruling house, a skill or art leads to debasement of status. Anyone who is especially skilled in a particular art is a technician, not a samurai. (Book One)

The Compromise Climate of Today, When One May Neither Live Beautifully Nor Die Horribly

'If your name means nothing to the world whether you live or die, it is better to live.' (Book One) This way of thinking did exist in the time of *Hagakure*, of course. The human instinct for survival, faced with a decision between life and death, normally forces us to choose life. But we must recognize that when a human being tries to live beautifully and die beautifully, strong attachment to life undermines that beauty. It is difficult to live and to die beautifully, but it is equally difficult both to live and to die in a thoroughly horrible way. This is the lot of mankind.

The compromise climate of the times arises from the fact that those who try to live beautifully and die beautifully are actually choosing an unsightly death, whereas those who wish to live horribly and die horribly are choosing a beautiful way of life. *Hagakure* pronounces a delightful verdict on this question of life and death. Here again is the most famous line in *Hagakure*: 'I found that the Way of the Samurai is death.' Jōchō goes on to say, 'In a life or death crisis, simply settle it by deciding on immediate death. There is nothing complicated about it. Just brace yourself and proceed.' (Book One)

The Ideal Love Is Undeclared

Hagakure also discusses romantic love – in fact, as Bunsō Hashikawa has pointed out, it is probably the only work in classical Japanese literature to develop a logical theory of romantic love.[1] The ideal presented in *Hagakure* may be summed up in one expression, 'secret love', and *Hagakure* maintains flatly that once love has been confessed, it shrinks in stature; true love attains its highest and noblest form when one carries its secret to the grave.

The art of romantic love as practised in America involves declaring oneself, pressing one's suit, and making the catch. The energy generated by love is never allowed to build up within but is constantly radiated outward. But paradoxically, the voltage of love is dissipated the instant it is transmitted. Contemporary youth are richly blessed with opportunities for romantic and sexual adventure that former generations would never have dreamed of. But at the same time, what lurks in the hearts of modern youth is the demise of what we know as romantic love. When romantic love generated in the heart proceeds along a straight path and repeats over and over again the process of achieving its goal and in that instant ceasing to exist, then the inability to love and the death of passions (a phenomenon peculiar to the modern age) is within sight. It is fair to say that this is the main reason that young people today are tormented by contradictions concerning the problem of romantic love.

Until the war, youths were able to distinguish neatly between romantic love and sexual desire, and they lived quite reasonably with both. When they entered the university, their upper-classmen took them to the brothels and taught them how to satisfy their desire, but they dared not lay a hand on the women they truly loved.

Thus love in prewar Japan, while it was based on a sacrifice in the form of prostitution, on the other hand preserved the old 'puritanical' [in English] tradition. Once we accept the existence of romantic love, we must also accept the fact that men must have in a separate place the sacrificial object with which to satisfy their carnal desires. Without such an outlet, true love cannot exist. Such is the tragic physiology of the human male.

Romantic love as seen by Jōchō is not strategy designed for the preservation of this half-modernized, role-differentiated, pragmatic, and flexible arrangement. It is always reinforced by death. One must die for love, and death heightens love's tension and purity. This is the ideal love for *Hagakure*.

Hagakure: Potent Medicine To Soothe the
Soul Suffering

As can be surmised from what I have already said, *Haga-kure* is an attempt to cure the peaceful character of modern society by the potent medicine of death. This medicine, during the hundred years of war preceding the Tokugawa Period, had been all too liberally resorted to in the daily lives of the people, but with the coming of peace, it was feared as the most drastic medicine and avoided. Jōchō Yamamoto's discovery is that this most drastic medicine contains an effective treatment for soothing the suffering spirit of man. The author, in his abundant understanding of human life, knows that man does not live by his life alone. He knows just how paradoxical is human freedom. And he knows that the instant man is given freedom he grows weary of it, and the instant he is given life he becomes unable to bear it.

Ours is an age in which everything is based on the premise that it is best to live as long as possible. The average life span has become the longest in history, and a monotonous plan for humanity unrolls before us. The youth's enthusiasm for 'my-home-ism' lasts as long as he is struggling to find his own little nest. As soon as he has found it, the future holds nothing for him. All there is is the retirement money clicked up in rows on the abacus, and the peaceful, boring life of impotent old age. This image is constantly in the shadow of the welfare state, threatening the hearts of mankind. In the Scandinavian countries, the need to work has by now disappeared, and there is no more worry over support in old age; in their boredom and disillusionment at being ordered by society simply to 'rest', an extraordinary number of old people commit suicide. And in England, which after the war reached the ideal standard of a welfare nation, the desire to work has been lost, and what follows is the crippling and decline of industry.

Suppressed, the Death Impulse Must Explode Eventually

In discussing the direction modern society should take, some people propose the ideal of socialism and others the ideal of the welfare state, but these two are actually one and the same. At the extremity of freedom is the fatigue and boredom of a welfare state; needless to say, at the extremity of a socialist state there is suppression of freedom. With one part of his heart man supports grand social 'visions' [in English], but then while he proceeds one step at a time, as soon as the idea seems attainable he becomes bored with it. Each and every one of us hides within his subconscious mind deep, blind impulses. These are the dynamic expression of the contradictions filling one's life from moment to moment, a manifestation that has essentially nothing to do with social ideals for the future. In youth these are manifested in their boldest, sharpest form. Moreover, such blind impulses appear in dramatic opposition, even in confrontation with one another. Youth possesses the impulse to resist and the impulse to surrender, in equal measure. One might re-define these as the impulse to be free and the impulse to die. The manifestation of these impulses, no matter how political the form it assumes, is like an electric current that results from a difference in electrical charge – in other words, from the fundamental contradictions of human existence.

During the war, the death impulse was 100 per cent liberated, but the impulse for resistance and freedom, for life, was completely suppressed. In the postwar age, this condition is exactly reversed, and whereas the impulse for resistance and freedom and life is 100 per cent fulfilled, the impulse for surrender and death is never fulfilled at all. About ten years ago in a conversation with a certain conservative politician, I said that perhaps the postwar Japanese government, in bringing about economic prosperity, had at least managed to fulfil the drive of modern youth for life, but I did not have the chance to talk about the drive for death. On another occasion, however, I have explained that we are constantly exposed to the danger that the death drive suppressed within modern youth will someday explode.

I believe that the battle over the renewal of the American Security Treaty is one instance of extreme difference in electrical charge. The Security Treaty struggle was politically complex, and the young people who participated in it were simply seeking a cause for which they would be willing to lay down their lives. They were not necessarily governed by ideology, and their conduct was not founded on their own reading of the text of the Security Treaty. They were trying to satisfy both their inner drives, the drives for resistance and death.

The frustration that followed the failure of the anti-Security Treaty demonstrations was even worse, however. Those who had participated were made to realize that the political movement to which they had devoted themselves was a sort of fiction, that death does not transcend reality, that political achievements provide no satisfaction, that the energy of all their actions had been in vain. Once again the youth in modern Japan received the crushing sentence, 'The cause for which you died was not worthwhile.'

As Toynbee says, the reason Christianity gathered so many avid converts so suddenly is because these people had fervently wished for a goal worth dying for. In the age of the Pax Romana, the lands under Roman domination, including all of Europe and extending even to Asia, enjoyed interminable peace. However, the only people who were able to avoid the boredom and fatigue that seep into an age of peace were the frontier guards. The frontier guards had found a goal worth dying for.

Times Have Changed

Hagakure is based on the principles of the samurai. The occupation of the samurai is death. No matter how peaceful the age, death is the samurai's supreme motivation, and if a samurai should fear or shun death, in that instant he would cease to be a samurai. It is for this reason that Jōchō Yamamoto puts such emphasis on death as his fundamental motivation to action. However, in present-day Japan under a constitution that outlaws war, people who consider death to be their occupational objective – and this includes the National Defense Force – cannot exist, on principle. The premise of the democratic age is that it is best to live as long as possible.

Thus in evaluating the impact of *Hagakure*, it becomes an important question whether or not the readers are samurai. If one is able to read *Hagakure* transcending the fundamental difference in premise between Jōchō's era and our own, one will find there an astonishing understanding of human nature, a wisdom applicable to human relations even in the present day. One reads lightly and quickly through its pages (stimulating, vigorous, passionate, but extremely sharp and penetrating, paradoxical pages), letting one's body be refreshed as by a spring rain. But in the end one is forced to confront again the fundamental difference in premise.

The reader, temporarily surmounting this difference in premise, comes to resonate with the text; then at the conclusion he must give way once more before the unresolvable difference. That is what is interesting about *Hagakure*.

The Significance of *Hagakure* for the Present Day

But what exactly is this difference? Here we transcend occupation, class discrimination, and the conditions ascribed to any individual in a specific era, and we are brought back to the basic problem of life and death, a problem we too must face in this day and age. In modern society the meaning of death is constantly being forgotten. No, it is not forgotten; rather, the subject is avoided. Rainer Maria Rilke (poet, born in Prague, 1875–1926) has said that the death of man has become smaller. The death of a man is now nothing more than an individual dying grandly in a hard hospital bed, an item to be disposed of as quickly as possible. And all around us is the ceaseless 'traffic war', which is reputed to have claimed more victims than the Sino-Japanese War, and the fragility of human life is now as it has ever been. We simply do not like to speak about death. We do not like to extract from death its beneficial elements and try to put them to work for us. We always try to direct our gaze towards the bright landmark, the forward-facing landmark, the landmark of life. And we try our best not to refer to the power by which death gradually eats away our lives. This outlook indicates a process by which our rational humanism, while constantly performing the function of turning the eyes of modern man towards the brightness of freedom and progress, wipes the problem of death from the level of consciousness, pushing it deeper and deeper into the subconscious, turning the death impulse by this repression to an ever more dangerous, explosive, ever more concentrated, inner-directed impulse. We are ignoring the fact that bringing death to the level of consciousness is an important element of mental health.

But death alone exists unchanged and regulates our lives now as in the era of *Hagakure*. In this sense, the death that

Jōchō is talking about is nothing extraordinary. *Hagakure* insists that to ponder death daily is to concentrate daily on life. When we do our work thinking that we may die today, we cannot help feeling that our job suddenly becomes radiant with life and meaning.

It seems to me that *Hagakure* offers us a chance to re-evaluate our views of life and death, after twenty years of peace since the Second World War.

Notes

1. Bunsō Hashikawa (1922–   ). Critic at large and scholar of modern Japanese intellectual history.

The Forty-eight Vital Principles
of *Hagakure*

Hagakure and Its Author, Jōchō Yamamoto

Human life lasts but an instant. One should spend it doing what one pleases. In this world fleeting as a dream, to lie in misery doing only what one dislikes is foolishness. (Book Two)

The Origin of the Title *Hagakure*

The title of the book we are calling *Hagakure* was originally and formally *Recorded Words of the Hagakure Master*, and has been abbreviated as *Hagakure*. The title first appeared on the original edition of the version by the transcriber and editor, Tsuramoto Tashiro. There have been many theories ventured over the years as to the significance of the word *hagakure*.[1] No clear conclusion has been reached, however.

Among various conjectures is the theory that it was chosen to convey the atmosphere of a poem by the priest Saigyō (poet-monk of the late Heian and early Kamakura periods),[2] included in the *Sanka wakashū*.[3] The poem is entitled 'Sent to a Lover When a Few Blossoms Linger':

> Only in the few blossoms lingering,
> Still hidden among the leaves,
> Do I seem to feel
> The presence of her
> For whom I secretly long.

A second theory holds that the title reflects the fact that *Hagakure* is in essence a book about self-sacrifice, about samurai service performed inconspicuously in the shadow, and that it was related and written down in Jōchō's secluded hut 'hidden among the leaves'.

Third is a theory which maintains that there must have been growing near Jōchō's hut a persimmon tree that bore such abundant fruit that it was named 'Leaf Hider', and he took the title from the name of his tree.

Here is a fourth theory. It is said that on the grounds of Saga Castle, the castle of the Nabeshima daimyo during the Tokugawa Period, there were many trees and the castle was given therefore the alias 'Leaf-hidden Castle', the samurai of the domain being called by extension the 'leaf-hidden samurai'. There are those who believe this to be the origin of the title *Hagakure*, but although Saga Castle has many large trees with luxuriant foliage along the edges of the moat so that the castle itself is wrapped in green, natives of Saga say they have never heard the castle called 'Leaf-hidden Castle', so this theory is merely one more piece of speculation.

The Background and Composition of *Hagakure*

Recorded Words of the Hagakure Master was originally a transcription of oral discussions. In the thirteenth year of Genroku [1700] a samurai of Saga Han[4] named Jōchō Yamamoto retired from worldly life after the death of his lieged lord, Mitsushige Nabeshima (the second daimyo of Saga Han), and after building a grass hut began a hermit's existence in a place in Saga called Kurotsuchiparu, remote from human society. Ten years later, in the spring of Hōei seven [1710], a young Saga samurai named Tsuramoto Tashiro called on Jōchō in his hut and wrote down what Jōchō told him. What Tashiro then spent seven years collecting and arranging into eleven volumes is what we know as *The Recorded Words of the Hagakure Master*. Jōchō ordered him to throw his records into the fire and burn them, but Tsuramoto Tashiro disobeyed him and secretly preserved what he had written, which in no time began to be copied and distributed among the samurai of Saga, who held great store by it, calling it 'The Analects of Nabeshima'.

Hagakure is not merely the record of random observations but a compilation with which great care has been taken, both in composition and arrangement. The composition is roughly as follows.

Volume One (*Recorded Words of the Hagakure Master*, Part One) and Volume Two (*Recorded Words of the Hagakure Master*, Part Two) are the teachings of Jōchō himself. Volumes Three, Four, and Five record the words and deeds of Naoshige Nabeshima (founder of the *han*), Katsushige (the first daimyo of Saga), Mitsushige, and Tsunashige (third daimyo of Saga) Nabeshima, respectively. Volumes Six through Nine deal with Saga Han and the words and deeds of her samurai. Volume Ten describes the exploits of samurai of other han, and Volume Eleven is a supplement to the other ten volumes.

The nucleus of the work is the account of Jōchō's own teachings, related in the first two volumes, where his philosophy of life is in vivid evidence. But the order of the discussions these two volumes contain is not necessarily chronological. *Hagakure* Volume One opens with the statement, 'In the seventh year of Hōei [1710], on the fifth day of the third month I first paid a respectful call ...' This refers to the memorable day when Tsuramoto Matazaemon Tashiro first visited the hut of Jōchō Yamamoto and listened to his lectures.

Jōchō had been in the attendance of Mitsushige, the second lord of the Nabeshima house, the hereditary feudal lords of Saga Han, and he had been in close attendance on this master from early childhood until his forty-second year. His ancestors for generations had served the Nabeshima house valiantly, and Jōchō himself was favoured with great trust by the daimyo. It would be natural to expect that at the age of fifty he would be named an elder of the han, one of the leaders of han government, but when he was forty-two the daimyo died and his ambitions were never fulfilled. Jōchō had determined to commit suicide in loyalty to his deceased master. But Mitsushige Nabeshima was ahead of his time in strictly forbidding such loyalty suicides in his domain, and he issued an edict to the effect that if anyone committed suicide upon his death, the honour of that man's family would be destroyed. In those days, when one valued the family above the individual, Jōchō was unable to commit suicide, deciding instead to retire from secular life. He lived in seclusion for twenty years, until his death at the age of sixty-one on the tenth day of the tenth month of Kyōhō four [1719]. It is said that *Recorded Words of the Hagakure Master* was begun in Jōchō's fifty-second year and covers seven years, ending on the tenth day of the ninth month of Kyōhō one [1716]. This work closely resembles Eckermann's *Conversations with Goethe* in that the sharp sensitivity and editorial skill of the listener, in other words, the transcriber, are extremely significant.

Jōchō and the Transcriber, Tsuramoto Tashiro

Tsuramoto Matazaemon Tashiro, who was employed as an official scribe, was a sturdy young man of thirty-two or thirty-three, twenty years the junior of Jōchō. As I have said before, the Genroku and Hōei periods – some eighty years having passed since the more austere periods of Keichō and Genna, while serious works on Confucianism, military art, and samurai conduct continued to be produced – were a time of renaissance exemplified by the haiku poetry of Bashō, the tragedies of Chikamatsu, and the fiction of Saikaku.[5] Not only the city merchants but even the samurai indulged themselves in the aesthetic pleasure of poetry, music, and dance. Manuals of samurai ethics, Confucian

tracts, and the military arts themselves tended to degenerate
into idle moral philosophizing. The originator of *Hagakure,* Jōchō Jin'emon Yamamoto, was born on Yoko-
kōji Street in the town of Katatae in Saga Han on the
eleventh day of the sixth month of Manji two [1659], and, as
I said before, he died at the age of sixty-one on the tenth
day of the eleventh month of Kyōhō four [1719]. To fill in
the details of his life, he was the youngest of two boys and
three girls born to Shigezumi Jin'emon Yamamoto. His
father, Jin'emon, was the younger brother of Kiyoaki Jin'-
emon Nakano and was adopted into the family of Muneharu
Sukebei Yamamoto. The name Jin-emon was given to him
by order of the daimyo, and Kiyoaki Nakano was the first
generation, Shigezumi Yamamoto the second, and Jōchō the
third to bear the name. These three came to be called the
three generations of Nakano.

Jōchō lost his father at the age of eleven, and, studying
under the tutelage of his cousin, Tsuneharu Gorozaemon
Yamamoto, twenty years his senior, received a general education. While he studied Confucianism and Buddhism under
Ittei Ishida and the Zen master Tannen, from an early age
he was in close attendance on the daimyo, so he could not
devote himself completely to academic pursuits. Then he
was strongly impressed by the Zen master Ryōi, and it is
felt that after his retirement from secular life he was initiated into the secrets of Zen through his profound appreciation of Ryōi's teachings.

Jōchō also had the usual understanding of the military
arts and at the age of twenty-four performed the function of
second (beheader) at his cousin's ritual suicide. He was also
skilled at composing haiku and waka poetry, and when he
was sent to Kyoto by the Daimyo Mitsushige, he received
there a diploma of the Secrets of Waka Old and New (*Waka
kokindenju*)[6] from Sanenori Nishisanjō[7] under whom he
often had the opportunity to study directly.

After his retirement, Jōchō called himself Jōchō Kyo-kuzan (Eternal Morning, Sunrise Mountain), he named his hut Chōyōken (Eaves of the Morning Sun), and lived in seclusion there with Ryōi. Later he changed the name Chōyōken to Sōjun (Hut of Long Religious Life). In August of Shōtoku three [1713], Mitsushige's widow, Reijuin, was buried in Kurotsuchiparu, where Jōchō was living, so out of deference he moved to Ōkoguma in the nearby village of Kasuga.

Jōchō was the author of a book entitled *A Collection of my Humble Opinions* (Gukenshū), which in the second month of Hōei five [1708], at the age of fifty, he wrote for the instruction of his adopted son, Gonnojo. Jōchō had two daughters, the first of whom died young. The other daughter married a man who was adopted into their family, but Jōchō survived both husband and wife.

Hagakure: Three Philosophies

The First Characteristic, 'A Philosophy of Action'

As I see it, *Hagakure* as a philosophical work has three major characteristics. First, it is a philosophy of action; second, it is a philosophy of love; third, it is a living philosophy.

As a philosophy of action, *Hagakure* values subjectivity, considers action to be the function of subjectivity, and makes death the conclusion of action. The philosophy of *Hagakure* creates a standard of action which is the most effective means of escaping the limitations of the self and becoming immersed in something greater. Nothing could be further removed from Machiavellian philosophies, in which an outsider arbitrarily combines element a and element b, or manipulates power a and power b. Jōchō's is exclusively a subjective philosophy, not an objective one. It is a philosophy of action, not of government.

Because during the war *Hagakure* was utilized for political indoctrination, some people still interpret the work in political terms, but there is absolutely nothing political about it. I suppose the argument changes if one interprets the samurai ethic as a political concept, but as I see it the main purpose of *Hagakure* is to show human beings in certain fixed conditions where to look for their guiding principles. These are teachings with a universality applicable to any age, no matter how conditions may change. And yet they are also full of practical knowledge gained by individuals through practical experience.

The Second Characteristic, 'A Philosophy of Love'

In the second place, *Hagakure* is a philosophy of love. The Japanese have a particular tradition concerning romantic love and have developed a special concept of romance [*ren'ai*]. In old Japan there existed a kind of passion with sexual overtones [*koi*] but no love [*ai*]. In the West from the age of the Greeks a distinction was made between eros (love) and agape (the love of God for mankind). Eros began as a concept of carnal desire but, gradually transcending this meaning, it entered the realm of *idea* (the highest concept attained through reason), where it was perfected in the philosophy of Plato. Agape is a spiritual love completely divorced from carnal desire, and it is agape that was introduced later as Christian love.

Accordingly in the European ideal of love, agape and eros were always treated as opposing concepts. Woman worship in medieval chivalry had at its base the cult of the Virgin Mary (eros), but it is also true that the highest ideal of chivalry was love as agape completely divorced from eros.

The early modern European ideals of patriotism also may be said to have agape at their source. Without much exaggeration we can say, however, that in Japan there is no such thing as love for one's country. There is no such thing as love for a woman. In the basic spiritual make-up of the Japanese, eros and agape are melded. When love for a woman or a young man is pure and chaste, it is no different from loyalty and devotion to one's ruler. This concept of love, which makes no distinction between eros and agape, was called 'falling in love with the Imperial family' [*renketsu no jō*] at the end of the Tokugawa Period and laid the emotional groundwork for emperor worship.

The prewar emperor system has collapsed, but the concept of love in the spiritual make-up of the Japanese people has not necessarily collapsed along with it. This concept is based on a firm belief that that which emanates from pure instinctive sincerity leads directly to an ideal to strive for, to die for if necessary. Jōchō's philosophy of love has its foundations here. Citing as an example the love of a man for another man, which in his day was regarded as a higher, more spiritual emotion than love for a woman, he maintains that the truest and most intense form of human love develops into loyalty and devotion to one's ruler.

The Third Characteristic, 'A Living Philosophy'

In the third place, *Hagakure* is a living philosophy. It is not a tightly structured, consistent logical system. Volumes One and Two alone, the portion devoted to Jōchō's teachings, abound in discrepancies and contradictions, and it often seems that one teaching is completely reversed by the next. The most famous *Hagakure* line, 'I discovered that the Way of the Samurai is death,' is immediately followed by a statement that seems at first glance contradictory but is intended as reinforcement: 'Human life lasts but an instant. One should spend it doing what one pleases. In this world fleeting as a dream, to live in misery doing only what one dislikes is foolishness. Since this may prove harmful if misinterpreted, it is a trade secret I have decided not to pass on to young men.' (Book Two) In other words, 'I discovered that the Way of the Samurai is death' is the initial stage of the argument, and the principle that 'Human life lasts but an instant. One should spend it doing what one pleases' is the second stage, beneath the surface of the first statement and at the same time beyond it. Here *Hagakure* clearly shows itself as a living philosophy that holds life and death as the two sides of one shield.

In a crisis of life or death, Jōchō recommends that we settle it by dying quickly, but he also maintains that one must think constantly about what things will be like fifteen years in the future. Such forethought will finally enable one to become a good samurai after the fifteen years have passed, and fifteen years will go by more quickly than a dream. This statement, too, seems at first glance a self-contradiction, but actually Jōchō had little respect for time. Time changes human beings, makes them inconsistent and opportunistic, makes them degenerate or, in a very few cases, improve. However, if one assumes that humanity is always facing death, and that there is no truth except from moment to moment, then the process of time does not merit the respect we accord it. And because time is insignificant, as one lives out those fifteen years that pass as quickly as a dream, as one thinks each day will be one's last, something will be accumulated from day to day and moment to moment, and this accumulation will enable one eventually to serve one's lord well. This is the basic principle of the philosophy of life that *Hagakure* teaches.

Next let me examine this living philosophy, taking up one by one in their original order the vital principles of *Hagakure,* so full of apparent contradictions, adding my own interpretations as I go along.

1. In Praise of Energy

Jōchō says in the preface to *Hagakure*, 'Leisurely Talks in the Shadow of Night':

I had never desired to attain buddhahood. Even if I were to die and be reborn again seven times, I neither expected nor wanted anything more than to be a Nabeshima samurai and to devote myself entirely to the Han. In a word, all that is necessary for a Nabeshima samurai is that he have the strength of will to bear on his shoulders total responsibility for the ruling house of his han. We are all human beings. Why should one man be inferior to another? Skill and training are of no use unless one has great confidence in oneself. And if one does not use it for the peace and prosperity of the ruling house, training amounts to nothing . . .

While praising extravagantly the virtue of modesty, *Hagakure* also made the significant point that human energy brings about great action according to the physical laws of energy. There is no such thing as an excess of energy. When a lion runs full tilt, under his feet the fields disappear; he may even pass by the prey he was chasing to the far end of the field. Why? Because he is a lion.

Jōchō saw that a similar driving force is the great source of energy of human action. If one restricts one's life by the virtue of modesty, daily samurai training will never produce a dynamic ideal of action which transcends that training. This reinforces the principle that one must have great confidence in oneself, and that one must shoulder the burden of one's ruling house. Like the Greeks, Jōchō knew the fascination, the majestic radiance, and the horror of what is called hubris.

2. Decision

I discovered that the Way of the Samurai is death. In a fifty-fifty life or death crisis, simply settle it by choosing immediate death. There is nothing complicated about it. Just brace yourself and proceed. Some say that to die without accomplishing one's mission is to die in vain, but this is the calculating, imitation samurai ethic of arrogant Osaka merchants.[8] To make the correct choice in a fifty-fifty situation is nearly impossible. We would all prefer to live. And so it is quite natural in such a situation that one should find some excuse for living on. But one who chooses to go on living having failed in one's mission will be despised as a coward and a bungler. This is the precarious part. If one dies after having failed, it is a fanatic's death, death in vain. It is not, however, dishonourable. Such a death is in fact the Way of the Samurai. In order to be a perfect samurai, it is necessary to prepare oneself for death morning and evening day in and day out. When a samurai is constantly prepared for death, he has mastered the Way of the Samurai, and he may unerringly devote his life to the service of his lord. (Book One)

'When a samurai is constantly prepared for death, he has mastered the Way of the Samurai' is the new philosophy discovered by Jōchō. If a man holds death in his heart, thinking that whenever the time comes he will be ready to die, he cannot possibly take mistaken action. When a man takes mistaken action, Jōchō believes it must be in failing to die at the proper time. The proper time does not come along often, however. The choice between life and death may come only once in a lifetime. Think of Jōchō himself: With what feelings did he greet death when after so many years of daily resignation he realized it would overtake him undramatically in bed at the age of sixty-one?

But Jōchō is concerned with death as a decision, not with natural death. He spoke not of resignation to death from illness, but of resolution to self-destruction. Death from illness is the work of Nature, whereas self-destruction has to do with a man's free will. And if the extreme manifestation of man's free will is the free will to die, Jōchō asks, then what is free will? Here is the typical Japanese view that being cut down in battle and committing ritual suicide are equally honourable; the positive form of suicide called *harakiri* is not a sign of defeat, as it is in the West, but the ultimate expression of free will, in order to protect one's honour. What Jōchō means by 'death' is the deliberate choice to die, and no matter how constrained the situation, when one breaks through the constricting forces by choosing to die, one is performing an act of freedom. This is, however, inevitably an idealized view of death, and Jōchō knows perfectly well that death does not often appear in such a pure and uncomplicated form. The formula death-equals-freedom is the ideal formula of the samurai. One must read between the lines to find Jōchō's deep-rooted nihilism: He knows that death is not necessarily like that.

3. 'Delicacy' [In English]

A man's world is a world of consideration for others. A man's social ability is measured by his consideration. Though the era of the samurai may at a glance seem a rough-and-tumble world, it operated precisely on a delicate modulation of consideration for one's fellow man much finer than exists today. Even on the subject of criticizing others, Jōchō preaches at length the virtue of care and 'delicacy'.

Reprimanding people and correcting their faults is important; it is actually an act of charity – the first requirement of samurai service. One must take pains to do it in the proper way. It is an easy matter to find strong points and shortcomings in another man's conduct; it is equally easy to criticize them. Most people seem to believe it a kindness to tell people things they do not want to hear, and if their criticisms are not taken to heart, well, then nothing more can be done. Such an approach is totally without merit. It produces results no better than if one had set out wilfully to insult and embarrass the man. It is simply a way of getting things off one's chest. Criticism must begin *after* one has discerned whether or not the person will accept it, *after* one has become his friend, shared his interests, and behaved in such a way as to earn his complete trust so that he will put faith in whatever one says. Then there is the matter of tact: One must devise the proper way to say it, and the proper moment – perhaps in a letter, perhaps on the way home from a pleasant gathering. One might start by describing one's own failures, and make him see what one is getting at without a word more than is necessary. First one praises his strength, taking pains to encourage him and put him in the right mood, make him as receptive to one's words as a thirsty man is to water. Then correct his faults. To criticize well is extremely difficult . . . (Book One)

Advice is free. We may be reluctant to lend a hundred yen, but we are no more reluctant to part with a bit of free advice than with water. Advice almost never functions as a social lubricant; eight or nine times out of ten it makes people lose face, crushes their will, and creates a grudge. Jōchō is well aware of this phenomenon. It behoves us all to reflect upon the seriousness and sensitivity with which he approaches the problem of giving advice. Here he is firmly grounded in his scathing, realistic evaluation of human psychology. Certainly Jōchō is not one of those optimistic, irresponsible sermonizers (who, after all, are the most ignorant of human character).

4. Putting Principles Into Practice

Jōchō also provides us with various useful hints on the fine points of daily life.

To yawn in public is disrespectful. When you suddenly feel the urge to yawn, stroke your forehead upwards towards your scalp and the yawn will subside. If that does not work, close your mouth and lick the inside of your lips – or else yawn discreetly into your sleeve or cover your mouth with your hand in order to be as inconspicuous as possible. The same policy applies to sneezes. If you do not attend carefully to such matters, you will look ridiculous. In addition there are many other ways in which you must be careful to restrain yourself.

It is advisable always to make plans the evening before and make a note of the schedule. This is one way of staying a step ahead of other people.

Stifling a yawn is a technique that may be put into practice today. I first read this passage during the war, and after that, whenever I felt a yawn coming I licked my upper lip and managed to suppress it. Particularly during the war, when anyone who yawned in the middle of an important lecture was sure to be severely reprimanded, what Jōchō taught me proved invaluable.

It is my practice every evening to go over in detail my plans for the following day, and I am careful to jot down then the necessary book titles, messages, names and telephone numbers, etc., so that my work will proceed smoothly the next day, with no extra energy on my part. This too is just one of the extremely practical lessons I have learned from *Hagakure*.

5. Tolerance

Jōchō is by no means severe in his criticism of others. He knows how to make allowances for shortcomings. The following is his comment on the subject:

A certain person is constantly preaching strict austerity, but I disagree. As the proverb says, 'Fish do not live in clear water.' It is the seaweed that provides fish with a hiding place in which to grow safely to maturity. It is because one sometimes overlooks details and does not lend an ear to minor complaints that those in one's service are able to live in peace. An understanding of this point is essential when considering the character and deportment of others. (Book One)

In the Tokugawa Period the government issued one sumptuary edict after another; and the samurai lived a life of extreme asceticism totally opposite to the great mass consumption of the present day. This asceticism persisted until relatively recently and was still subscribed to during the war.

It was thought that morality consisted of suppressing one's taste for luxury and being as frugal as possible. Thanks to the postwar industrialization process, the age of mass consumption has arrived and it seems that this characteristic virtue of the Japanese has been swept away forever.

In comparison with the arbitrary, restrictive morality of Japanese Confucianism, *Hagakure* maintains from the first a liberal, tolerant point of view. The *Hagakure* philosophy, which stresses the virtue of spontaneous action and bold decision, is a far cry from the bureaucratic ethic of frugality of palace maids inspecting the corners of a lacquer container to salvage one last grain of rice. And as an extrapolation of the consideration for others he preaches, Jōchō recommends deliberately overlooking or closing one's ears to the misses and shortcomings of underlings. Such a philosophy of conscious oversight has always lived in the hearts of the Japanese, at once contradicting and reinforcing their punctilious, ceremonious frugality. Nowadays the proper bounds of overlooking and not hearing have been overstepped, and pretending not to notice has taken precedence over economy, resulting in a moral decay sometimes referred to as 'the black fog'. This is not tolerance; it is merely laxity. Only when they are founded on strict rules of morality can overlooking and pretending not to hear qualify as human virtues; when these morals have collapsed, overlooking and not hearing may become inhuman vices.

6. Women

Jōchō expresses very few opinions on the subject of women. He says:

. . . Most important, a woman must think of her husband as her liege lord. (Book One)

On several points *Hagakure* resembles the philosophy of the Greeks, particularly the Spartans. In ancient Greece the wife served the hearth god, remained always in the home, and was expected to devote herself to the care of her children and the house and to respect her husband. The man, however, went out and had love affairs with beautiful young men, or disported himself with prostitutes or his educated concubine-slaves, the *hetaera*. This is a good approximation of Jōchō's views on women.

7. Nihilism

The Chinese character *gen* (幻) can be read in Japanese as *maboroshi* and means 'illusion'. In Japanese, Indian magicians are called *genshutsushi* (幻出師), or 'illusionists'. Human beings in this life are like marionettes. That is why one uses the character *gen*, to suggest the 'illusion' of free will. (Book One)

Jōchō frequently refers to this life as a puppet existence, to human beings as marionettes. At the very core of his personality is a deep, penetrating and yet manly 'nihilism' [in English]. He scrutinizes each moment to extract the meaning of life, but at heart he is convinced that life itself is nothing more than a dream.

I will elaborate on Jōchō's nihilism later, in connection with another passage.

8. The Objectivity of Righteousness

To hate evil and live one's life in righteousness is exceedingly difficult. Surprisingly enough, many errors arise from believing that it is essential to be strictly logical and to value righteousness above all else. There is a way more lofty than righteousness, but discovering it is no easy matter and requires wisdom of the highest order. Compared to this Way, logical principles are insignificant indeed. What one has not experienced firsthand one cannot know. And yet, there is a means of learning the truth even though one has not been able to discern it for oneself. The way lies in talking with other people. It is often true that even a person who has not yet perfected himself may be able to give direction to others. The principle involved is similar to what in *go* is called 'the advantage is to the onlooker'. One speaks of 'learning one's faults through contemplation', but this too is best done by talking with others. The reason is that when one learns by listening to what others have to say and by reading books, one transcends the limitations of one's own powers of discernment and follows the teachings of the ancients. (Book One)

In this passage on the relative character of righteousness, *Hagakure* approaches the political doctrine of democracy. It is a principle of democracy that in order to ascertain the righteousness of one's beliefs, one must await the judgement of a third person. While advocating a dynamic philosophy of action, Jōchō always leaves some doubt as to the righteousness of the conduct itself. Purity of action is the purity of subjectivity. But if action can be based on righteousness, one must be able to test the purity of its righteousness by another method; in other words, by an objective standard. Although one may judge the purity of an action by the action itself, Jōchō realizes that the purity of righteousness must be measured differently. The proper method is consultation. The principle behind the saying, 'The advantage is to the onlooker', can save people who are addicted to one brand of righteousness. Here *Hagakure* takes an ideologically relativistic point of view.

9. How to Run Your Life

Among the public proclamations of Lord Naoshige is the following: 'One should take important considerations lightly.' A commentary by Ittei Ishida (Confucian scholar of Saga Han, and Jōchō Yamamoto's teacher) explains, 'Small matters should be taken seriously.' Truly important problems are few; they occur probably no more than twice or thrice in a lifetime. Everyday reflection will tell you this. Therefore it is necessary to plan ahead what to do in case of a crisis, and then when the time comes, to remember the plan and dispose of the problem accordingly. Without daily preparation, when faced with a difficult situation one may be unable to reach a quick decision, with disastrous results. Therefore, may we not say that daily resolution upon a certain course of action is the principle behind the statement, 'One should take important considerations lightly'? (Book One)

Belief is resolution. Resolution must be tested daily over many years. Apparently, Jōchō makes a distinction between major beliefs and minor beliefs. In other words, one must nurture major beliefs in one's daily life so that at the moment of decision to act they may be carried out effortlessly, spontaneously. Minor beliefs are the philosophy that governs the trivia of day-to-day existence. Prosper Mérimée (nineteenth-century French novelist, historian, and philologist) once remarked that 'In fiction there must be a theoretical basis to the most minute details. Even a single glove must have its theory.' This is true not only of novelists: While we live and enjoy life, we must always approach even the smallest matters theoretically, exercising our judgement and making decisions. Otherwise, the framework of our life collapses, and sometimes even our greatest beliefs are violated. When Englishmen drink tea, the pourer always asks each person whether he prefers 'milk first' or 'tea first'. One might suppose that it comes to the same thing whether it is the milk or the tea that is poured into the cup first, but in this seemingly rather trivial matter the English ideology of life is staunchly in evidence. Certain Englishmen are convinced that milk should be poured into the teacup first, then the tea, and if one were to reverse the order, doubtless they would see the act as the first step to violation of the principles they hold most dear.

What Jōchō means by 'One should take important considerations lightly' is that, as a tiny ant-hole may cause a dike to collapse, one must pay attention to the little theories that govern our daily life waking and sleeping, the minor beliefs. This is a good lesson for our perverted day and age, in which only ideology is valued and the trifling practices of everyday life are not taken seriously.

10. Preparation and Decision

The major beliefs, to which one must be resolved day in and day out, are founded on the principle that one must die according to the Way of the Samurai.

. . . Among other things, the Way of the Samurai requires that he realize that something may occur at any moment to test the depth of his resolution, and day and night he must sort out his thought and prepare a line of action. Depending on the circumstances, he may win or lose. But avoiding dishonour is quite a separate consideration from winning or losing. To avoid dishonour he must die. But if the first time things do not proceed as he would wish, he must try again. For this he needs no special wisdom or skill. The veteran samurai thinks not of victory or defeat but merely fights insanely to the death . . . (Book One)

It is because the preparation has been long that a decision may be quickly reached. One may choose a course of action, but one may not always choose the time. The moment of decision looms in the distance and then overtakes you. Then is to live not to prepare for that moment of decision, chosen for one from afar, possibly by fate? Jōchō emphasizes the importance of disciplining oneself to act when the moment of fate arrives.

11. Constant Resignation to the Perpetual Threat of Death

Hagakure goes on to explain in greater detail the ideas expressed in Passages Nine and Ten.

Until fifty or sixty years ago, samurai performed their ablutions every morning, shaved their heads, and perfumed their topknots. Then they cut their fingernails and toenails, filed them with pumice, and finally buffed them with *kogane* herb. They were never lazy about such matters but took great care to be well groomed. Then a samurai took a look at his long and short swords to make sure that they were not rusting, wiped off the dust, and polished them. Taking such pains over one's appearance may seem foppish, but the custom did not arise from a taste for elegance or romance. One may be run through at any moment in vigorous battle; to die having neglected one's personal grooming is to reveal a general sloppiness of habit, and to be despised and mocked by the enemy. So in youth as in old age samurai took pains to look their best. Such fastidiousness may seem time consuming and more trouble than it is worth, but it is what the Way of the Samurai is all about. Actually, it takes little trouble or time. If, always prepared to die, a samurai begins to think of himself as already dead, if he is diligent in serving his lord and perfects himself in the military arts, surely he will never come to shame; but if a samurai spends his days selfishly doing exactly as he pleases, in a crisis he will bring dishonour upon himself. Having done so, he will not even be aware of his shame, and imagining that as long as he is secure and happy nothing else matters, he will disport himself unspeakably – a thoroughly lamentable development.

A samurai who is not prepared to die at any moment will inevitably die an unbecoming death. But a samurai who lives his life in constant preparation for death – how can he conduct himself in a despicable manner? One should reflect well on this point and behave accordingly. Times have changed in the last thirty years. Now when young samurai get together they talk of money, of profit and loss, how to run a household efficiently, how to judge the value of clothing, and they exchange stories about sex. If any other topic is mentioned, the atmosphere is spoiled and everyone present feels vaguely uncomfortable. What a distressing pass things have come to! It used to be that until the age of twenty or thirty a young man never thought a mean or worldly thought, and so of course he never spoke of such things. And if in their presence older men by accident should let such a remark escape their lips, young men felt as afflicted by it as if they had been physically wounded. Apparently the new trend has arisen because the modern age has come to value luxury and ostentation. Money alone has come to assume great importance. (Book One)

12. Proper Behaviour at a Drinking Party

The disorderliness of Japanese drinking parties is internationally notorious. Possibly the Japanese have a lower capacity for alcohol, but there is also a difference in outlook. It is considered unforgivable in the West for a gentleman to become intoxicated and behave in an unseemly way at a drinking party. Society regards alcoholics as failures and outcasts, and one may see them with wine bottle in hand, staggering like ghosts, on street corners frequented only by alcoholics.

In Japan there is a strange convention by which ordinary human beings strip themselves of their dignity when they drink, exposing their weaknesses and baring their hearts, confessing the most embarrassing secrets. No matter how they grumble or whine, they are completely forgiven on the excuse that they have been drinking. I do not know how many bars there are in Shinjuku, but in that overwhelming number of bars 'salary men' sit and drink and complain about women and their bosses. The bar becomes a small, miserable, secret-revealing place protected by the tacit mutual promise that in the morning, although they have not actually forgotten, they will pretend to have forgotten the unmanly, sloppy confessions exchanged among friends the night before.

In other words, the drinking party in Japan is a public gathering where one is exposed to the eyes of others but pretends that one is in private. Though people listen, they pretend not to hear; and though what is said may be painful to the ear, the listener pretends to be unaffected, and all is forgiven in the name of alcohol. But *Hagakure* warns that all drinking parties take place 'in the open air', by which he means exposed to the public. Though a samurai may attend a party where alcohol is served, he must restrain himself. This teaching is surprisingly like the English ideal of 'gentlemanship' [in English].

Many men have failed in life as a result of overdrinking. This is exceedingly unfortunate. One must know one's capacity for drink, and it is advisable never to drink more. Even so, one occasionally miscalculates. A samurai must never relax his guard when drinking, so that if ever something unexpected should occur he will be able to deal with it appropriately. Banquets where alcohol is served are like the open air, and there are many observing eyes. One must be careful. (Book One)

That Jōchō needed to make such a point, however, is simply an indication that then as now it was the general rule not to behave discreetly when drinking.

13. A Morality of Appearances

Ruth Benedict (American anthropologist, 1887–1948) in her well-known book *The Chrysanthemum and the Sword* defines Japanese morality as 'a morality of shame'. There are various problems with this definition, but it is quite natural that the Way of the Samurai should value external appearances. A warrior is constantly mindful of his enemies. The samurai has no choice but to defend his honour and his morale by constant anticipation: 'Will I not be shamed before my enemies? Will my enemies not despise me?' The samurai's conscience takes the form of the enemy itself. Thus, the essential characteristic of *Hagakure* is not an introspective morality but a morality concentrating on external reflection. In light of the history of ethical thought, it is not at all clear which of these two, internally or externally oriented morality, has proved more effective. Let us look at Christianity. The Catholics, who entrust their moral authority to the Church, are on relatively secure ground psychologically, whereas for the Protestants, the individual conscience must bear responsibility for the soul. Many weak men have been crushed under the weight of this intolerable moral burden, as one may see in the United States, where there are numberless mental patients suffering from severe neuroses.

To quote *Hagakure*:

When calling on a friend who has met with a personal disaster, what one says to him by way of encouragement is extremely important. He will be able to read one's real motives in these words. A true samurai must never seem to flag or lose heart. He must push on courageously as though sure to come out on top. Otherwise he is utterly useless. Here is the secret of encouraging a friend in trouble. (Book One)

'A true samurai must never seem to flag or lose heart.' This remark suggests that it is a defect to *seem* to flag, to *seem* disheartened. The most important thing is that a samurai not manifest externally his disappointment or his fatigue.

It is natural for any human being to become dispirited and worn out, and samurai are no exception. However, morality asks one to do the impossible. And the samurai ethic is a political science of the heart, designed to control such discouragement and fatigue in order to avoid showing them to others. It was thought more important to look healthy than to be healthy, and more important to seem bold and daring than to be so. This view of morality, since it is physiologically based on the special vanity peculiar to men, is perhaps the supreme male view of morality.

14. A Philosophy of Extremism

As was mentioned in Passage One, once we have admitted the appropriateness of energy as the motivating principle of action, then we can do nothing but follow the physical laws of energy. A lion can only run headlong to the far end of an open field. That is the way a lion proves that he is a lion. Jōchō thinks that going to excess is an important spiritual 'springboard' [in English]. One sees this attitude clearly in the following passage.

The Golden Mean is greatly valued, but when it comes to the martial arts, even in daily practice a samurai must constantly feel that his skill surpasses that of everyone else. In archery we have target practice. If one aims directly at the guidelines on the target, however, the arrow will tend to drift to the right and upward. The solution is to aim low and to the left. Then the arrow will hit its mark.

A samurai whose object is to excel on the battlefield, surpassing men of great military prowess, a samurai who spends his days and nights devising ways to capture a strong enemy, is the personification of samurai valour, vigorous and indomitable. So say the brave old warriors' tales. In daily life, too, such must be one's resolution. (Book One)

15. The Education of Children

Though England and America are both Anglo-Saxon societies, they educate their children quite differently. According to the traditional upbringing of English children, they are rarely allowed to appear in the presence of adults, and when they are, they must remain absolutely silent. Moreover, they must not disrupt the grown-ups' conversation by speaking among themselves. Silence is enforced upon a child as part of the social training he must undergo in order to be prepared to speak as a proper gentleman later in life.

According to the American way of bringing up children, children are in fact required to participate actively in conversations, for the sake of their social training. Adults listen to children's conversation, adults and children have discussions together, and a child is thus expected from an early age to put forth his own opinion proudly.

It is not for me to say here which of these two approaches to child raising is correct. However, let me cite what *Hagakure* has to say on the subject:

There is an established formula for raising a samurai child. In infancy his courage is stimulated, and no one must ever threaten or deceive him. If even as a child he suffers from anxiety or fears, the defect will be a scar he carries to his grave. A child should not be allowed to become frightened of thunder through the oversight of his parents, or forbidden to go into the dark, and it is bad policy to tell him frightening stories to keep him quiet when he cries.

On the other hand, if he is scolded too severely as a child, he will grow into a shy, introverted adult. In any event one must take care that he does not acquire bad character traits. Once he has picked up an unfortunate trait, you will not rid him of it no matter how you lecture him. In speech and in etiquette he should be made to reach a general understanding of propriety, and he should never know vulgar desires. All others points are less important, since more normal, healthy children will grow up anyway regardless of their upbringing. It is of course true that children of a disharmonious marriage will be lacking in filial piety. Even the birds and beasts are influenced by what they see and hear from the moment they are born; one must be exceedingly careful about a child's environment. Sometimes things go badly between father and son because of a mother's foolishness. If a mother dotes unreasonably on her child and invariably takes the child's side when the father tries to scold him, she is forming a conspiracy with the child, which causes further friction between father and son. Conspiring with the child against the father apparently stems from a woman's natural shallowness of purpose and her calculation that by winning the favour of her son early in life she will ensure her well-being in years to come. (Book One)

Jōchō's method of education bears surprising resemblance to the ideal of free, natural education set forth in Rousseau's *Emile*. I might mention that the year *Hagakure*, begun in Hōei seven [1710], was first circulated in manuscript was 1711, the year that Rousseau was born.

What Jōchō advocates is not simply a Spartan education; he emphasizes the importance of keeping the child from developing a fear of nature, and of avoiding unreasonably harsh scolding. If children are allowed to grow up freely in a child's world without being threatened or unduly punished by their parents, they will not become cowardly or introverted. It is interesting to note that *Hagakure* goes on to cite a specific case in terms applicable to the present day. Today, too, mothers are in evidence everywhere who love their sons unreasonably and take sides with them against their fathers, with the result that the father–son relationship is disharmonious. Especially today, with the decline in the father's authority, the 'mother's darling' has become increasingly more common and there has been a dramatic rise in the number of what the Americans call the 'domineering mother type' [in English]. The father is ostracized, and the strict samurai instruction that is supposed to be handed down from father to son is completely neglected (indeed, there is no longer anything to hand down), and even for the child the father is reduced to a machine that brings home a pay-cheque. There is no spiritual bond between them. The feminization of men is a common object of criticism today. But one should realize that the weakening of the father's role is proceeding at an equally alarming rate.

16. Sincerity in Human Relations

The 'delicacy' [in English] of *Hagakure* also teaches that sincerity is the most important requisite for human relations. That view is accepted even today, with little opposition.

It is said, 'If you want to see into the heart of a friend, fall ill.' A person who is friendly to you in good times and turns his back on you like a stranger in times of illness or misfortune is a coward. It is most important when a friend has met with ill-fortune, to stand by him, to visit him, and to take him what he needs. A samurai must never as long as he lives permit himself to be cut off from those to whom he is spiritually indebted. Here is a standard for evaluating a man's true feelings. But most of the time we turn to others for help in times of trouble and forget them entirely when the crisis has passed.

17. The Proper Time to Fire a Servant

On the subject of employing servants, *Hagakure* offers us another bit of scrupulous but gentle advice:

Zenjin'emon Yamamoto (Jōchō's father), when one of his servants committed an impropriety, would continue to keep him in his service for the rest of the year as though nothing had happened and then calmly give him his leave just before the new year. (Book One)

18. Man and Mirror

As I have said before, if it is proper to emphasize the external aspect of morality, then this external aspect is best reflected by the enemy, and by the mirror. That which scrutinizes and evaluates one's behaviour is the enemy, and also the mirror. For a woman the mirror is a tool to be used in her daily toilette, but for a man the mirror is material for introspection.

In order to perfect his looks and his bearing, a samurai should make a habit of correcting them by looking in the mirror. When I reached the age of thirteen I bound my hair into the traditional topknot, but then I remained secluded at home for about a year. I did this because everyone in the family was saying, 'He has such a clever face that he is sure to wind up a failure. What the daimyo dislikes above all else is a person who looks intelligent.' So, determining to correct my facial expressions, I looked in the mirror day in and day out. After a year had passed and I reappeared everyone remarked that I looked somehow not very healthy, and I thought to myself, this is what samurai service is all about. There is something that makes one hesitate to trust a man who shows his intelligence in his face. If a man's bearing lacks a sense of calm dignity and serenity, one cannot call it handsome. A reverent yet stern, self-collected appearance is ideal. (Book One)

This is a strange example – the man whose face is too intelligent and who finally manages to correct his fault after much time spent looking in the mirror. But what *Hagakure* has to say here about ideal human, or rather manly, beauty – 'reverent yet stern, self-collected' – is still one kind of aesthetic for manly appearance. 'Reverent' requires a humility that inspires trust in others, while 'sternness' hints at an air of austerity and aloofness. What is needed to reconcile and bind together these two opposite elements is a serene, unflappable calm.

19. On Intellectuals

A calculating man is a coward. I say this because calculations all have to do with profit and loss, and such a person is therefore constantly preoccupied with profit and loss. To die is a loss, to live a gain, and so one decides not to die. Therefore one is a coward. Similarly a man of education camouflages with his intellect and eloquence the cowardice or greed that is his true nature. Many people do not realize this. (Book One)

In the age of *Hagakure*, probably there was no status corresponding to that of the modern 'intelligentsia' [in English]. However, their prototypes, the Confucianists, scholars, and the samurai themselves, began to form a similar class in an age of extended peace. Jōchō terms these simply 'calculating men'. He reveals in a word the vice that rationalism and humanism conceal. According to the deception of logic, death is loss, life is gain. Thinking rationally, who would be happy to go to his death? Humanism takes as its philosophical armour the humanism on which it is founded, and the humanist, under the illusion that he has achieved universality, hides beneath this armour the weakness of the self and the flimsiness of his subjective viewpoint. What Jōchō is continually criticizing is the discrepancy between subjectivity and philosophy. If philosophy is based on calculation, and if by calculating death as debit, life as credit, and if through cleverness and rhetoric one conceals one's inner cowardice and greed, then one is deceiving oneself with a philosophy one has devised, laying bare the pitiful image of a human being who has deceived himself.

Even according to modern humanism, one attains heroism when one wagers not the life of another but one's own life. In its most degenerate form, however, modern humanism is used to mask under the guise of sympathy for the death of another the animal reaction, 'I don't want to die,' and the self-interest of a person who intends to use such philosophy for his own benefit. This is what Jōchō means by cowardice.

20. Mania for Death

At the opposite extreme from the philosophical deception described in the previous passage lies an explosion of pure action, a spontaneous explosion without the aid of the abstract principles of loyalty to the daimyo, filial piety, etc. Jōchō is not simply endorsing fascism. His ideal is the purest form of action, which automatically subsumes the virtues of loyalty and filial piety. A samurai cannot predict beforehand whether his own actions will come to embody loyalty and filial piety. But human action does not always take a predictable course. The following passage, called 'The Way of the Samurai is a mania for death', is relevant.

Lord Naoshige said, 'The Way of the Samurai is a mania for death. Sometimes then men cannot topple a man with such conviction.' One cannot accomplish feats of greatness in a normal frame of mind. One must turn fanatic and develop a mania for dying. By the time one develops powers of discernment it is already too late to put them into effect. In the Way of the Samurai loyalty and filial piety are superfluous; all one needs is a mania for death. Within that attitude loyalty and filial piety will come to reside. (Book One)

In this anti-idealism, or anti-intellectualism if you prefer, there are inherent dangers. However, the greatest drawback

of idealism and intellectualism is that one does not offer
oneself up bravely in the face of danger. If intellect were automatically present in blind action, or if reason, just like instinct,
were to become a natural motivating force, the ideal form of
human action would result. One line quoted above, 'Within
that attitude loyalty and filial piety will come to reside,' is
vital. For Jōchō believes not in simple fanaticism, nor again
in simple anti-idealism, but in pre-ordained harmony of pure
action itself (a theory that the world is ordained by God
from the beginning of time to function in harmony).

21. Words and Deeds Alter the Heart

It is a common mistake these days to believe that words and
deeds are the manifestations of conscience and philosophy,
which in turn are the product of mind or heart. It is our
common error to believe in the existence of heart or mind,
conscience, thought, and abstract ideas, even when they are
not directly revealed in conduct. However, for a people like
the Greeks who trusted only in what they could see with
their own eyes, this invisible heart or mind does not exist at
all. And in order to manipulate that vague entity which is
the mind or the heart, if one wants to know what has nur-
tured it and changed it, one has no choice but to speculate
on the basis of external evidence, from a person's words and
actions. This is Jōchō's message. And he is warning us never
to utter a cowardly remark even in casual conversation.
Cowardly words make the heart itself cowardly, and being
regarded as a coward by others is the same as being a
coward. The slightest flaw in word or deed causes the collapse of one's philosophy of life. This can be a hard truth to
bear. If we believe in the existence of the heart or mind, in
order to protect it, we must watch what we say or do. By
taking meticulous care over the slightest word or deed, one
will become unimaginably rich in new-found inner passion,
and the heart will bear undreamed-of fruit.

A samurai must be careful in all matters, and he must strictly avoid even minor failures. Sometimes a samurai does not watch his tongue and inadvertently makes a remark such as, 'I am a coward', 'If that happens, let's run for our lives', 'How terrifying', or 'Ouch'. Such words must never pass one's lips, not in jest, nor in fun, nor asleep, nor by accident, not in any context whatsoever. A perceptive person hearing such a remark will discern one's true nature. One must always be on one's guard. (Book One)

22. Personal Advancement

Although seeming to recommend dying at the earliest possible moment, in practice Jōchō values the late bloomer. He seems to hint that human action and strength do not always come to flower at the same time as practical skills. This is because being in service has two meanings for the samurai. The first is to give up his life for his daimyo; the second is to serve the *han* with practical skill. It is an interesting aspect of *Hagakure* that it rates equally high both action and practical talent, commonly thought to be unrelated kinds of ability. Jōchō sees them as the two greatest kinds of ability, differentiating between them not in quality but according to the age of the individual concerned. One must recognize here the practical nature of *Hagakure*.

If one advances in the world as a young man one will not be effective in the service of one's daimyo. No matter how clever the samurai may be by birth, his abilities are not fully developed when he is young and he will not be sufficiently accepted by others. When he has reached the age of fifty, he must gradually finish his preparation. Behaving in such a way that most people believe his entering into public life is if anything slower than it should be, is actually the true way to commit himself to service. And even though he may ruin his fortunes, a man with the proper will has not done it by attempting wrongful gains to himself, and so he will recover it all in time. (Book One)

23. More Advice on Employing Servants

Here too is an extremely practical bit of advice:

In a *waka* about Yoshitsune[9] is the following statement: 'A general must speak often to the rank and file.' The people who serve in one's household, similarly, will be ready to devote their lives to one's service willingly if not merely in extraordinary circumstances but also on a regular basis one offers them such personal comments as, 'How well you have served me,' 'You must take the greatest care on this point,' 'Now here is a real veteran.' Such remarks are all-important.

24. Spiritual Concentration

This passage is clearly in contradiction with Passage Twenty-seven below. Specifically, although it is proper to concentrate one's energies single-mindedly on the Way of the Samurai, Jōchō despises 'the performing arts' as foolish pastimes, and he admonishes us not to concentrate our energies on them. The compound 'performing arts' [*geinō*] is used in *Hagakure* in a sense slightly different from its modern meaning. In the broadest sense, it means technical accomplishments, and it includes the skill of what today is called a technician. What I think Jōchō means is that a samurai is a total human being, whereas a man who is completely absorbed in his technical skill has degenerated into a 'function' [in English], one cog in a machine. One who devotes one's life wholeheartedly to the Way of the Samurai does not become the devotee of a particular skill and does not allow oneself to be treated as a simple function. A samurai must perform his duties so that as an individual he represents all samurai and his conduct in any given situation may stand for the Way of the Samurai. When a samurai prepares himself mentally to bear single-handedly the burden of the whole *han,* when he applies himself to his work with great self-confidence, he ceases to be a mere function. He is a *samurai*; he is the Way of the Samurai. There is no fear that such a human being will degenerate into a mere cog in the social machine. However, a man who lives for his technical proficiency cannot fulfil his total human role; all he can do is perform the single function, especially in a technology-oriented society such as ours. If a samurai who cherishes a total human ideal gives himself over to a particular talent or skill, his whole ideal will be eaten away by his specific function. This is what Jōchō fears. His image of the ideal human being is not a compromise product, one part function to one part total being. A total person does not need a skill. He represents spirit, he represents action, and he represents the ideal principles on which his realm is founded. That must be the meaning of the statement in the following passage.

It is wrong to set one's mind on two things at once. One must devote all one's energy to the Way of the Samurai; one must seek for nothing more. The same principle applies to the character for 'way' (道). However, one who has studied Confucianism or Buddhism may feel that the Way of the Samurai is an unreasonable 'way'. Only if you study all the various 'ways' will you eventually become able to understand what is truly reasonable. (Book One)

25. The Language of a Peaceful Era

One who in wartime employs rough and manly words appropriate to an age of war and in time of peace words appropriate to peacetime, is not a samurai. It is essential for a samurai to maintain logical consistency, and if one must show valour in one's action during times of chaos, then one must demonstrate equal valour in words during a peaceful age. This principle reinforces the belief, expressed in Passage Twenty-one, that a man's words and deeds determine his inner heart.

The first thing a samurai says on any occasion is extremely important. He displays with one remark all the valour of the samurai. In times of peace it is language that manifests valour. Even in times of chaos and destruction, great bravery may be revealed in a single word. One might say that this one word is a flower of the heart. (Book One)

26. Never a Word of Weakness

This passage is based on the same principle as Passages Twenty-one and Twenty-five:

Even in casual conversation, a samurai must never complain. He must constantly be on guard lest he should let slip a word of weakness. From a slight remark uttered inadvertently, one's true nature may be guessed. (Book One)

27. Contempt for Technical Skill

We have already discussed this point in Passage Twenty-four:

A man who earns a reputation for being skilled at a technical art is idiotic. Because of his foolishness in concentrating his energies on one thing, he has become good at it by refusing to think of anything else. Such a person is of no use at all. (Book One)

28. Imparting and Receiving Moral Instruction

It is strikingly characteristic of Japanese society that one is bound by the hierarchy of senior before junior and there is no opportunity for equal discussion between people of different ages; this is true of human relations today as well as in the past. Young people who have reluctantly accepted the instruction of their elders no longer have the opportunity to receive instruction by the time they themselves are in a position to instruct their juniors. Thus spiritual stagnation begins, 'arteriosclerosis' sets in, and the result is large-scale resistance to social change. Strangely enough, in Japan, even in recent history, it is only during periods of chaos and disruption that the opinions of youth have been respected; when peace reigns, they are ignored. The Red Guard in China was a thrilling stimulus to modern Japanese youth. Moreover, it is only extremely rarely that the opinions of young people are skilfully manipulated and put to practical use so that they will become a 'plus' [in English] in society. The Red Guard disturbances are one example; another is the ideology of young military officers in Japan from the mid-thirties until the Second World War, which in the end was utilized for wrong-headed political purposes. Only once in the history of the modern era have the ideas of young men swayed the main fortress of the state, served in fact in its creation. This was during the Meiji Restoration.

Many people give advice, but those who receive it gratefully are few. Still rarer are those who follow such advice. Once a man passes the age of thirty, there is no one to advise him. When advice ceases to reach him, he becomes wilful and selfish. For the rest of his life he adds impropriety to foolishness until he is beyond redemption. Therefore, it is absolutely necessary to find someone who knows what is right, to become well acquainted with him, and to receive his instruction. (Book One)

Here Jōchō is exhibiting his own brand of 'realism' [in English], and while carrying on at such great length in dictating *Hagakure*, he does not forget to add the comment, 'Those who accept advice gratefully are few.'

29. Harmony and Humility

Here Jōchō contradicts himself again. So lavish in his praise of energy and so blatant in approving excess, Jōchō surprisingly enough extols the virtues of harmony and humility.

... If one puts the other person before oneself, and without jealousy or competitiveness behaves according to etiquette, if one humbly thinks of the other person's interests even to one's personal disadvantage, each meeting will be as the first, and the relationship will never degenerate. (Book One)

When Jōchō gives us such bits of random practical advice, he often contradicts himself most shamelessly. This is part of the strange charm of *Hagakure*.

30. Age

Until the age of forty a samurai should not be carried away by wisdom or judgement but should depend on ability and strength. The stronger he is, the better. It depends on the individual and his status in life, but even after forty a samurai carries little weight without strength of character. (Book One)

The subject is strength. The point of this passage is that strength is everything in youth, but even after forty one cannot do without it. Apparently, Jōchō's image of humanity rests on the idea of 'strength'.

What is 'strength'? It is not to be carried away by attempts at wisdom. It is not to go overboard in judgement. Jōchō knew what it was like to watch patiently while his motivation to action was crushed by wisdom and judgement. And he had seen many people lose their strength as they reached the age of discernment, so that even their newly gained wisdom and judgement were rendered ineffectual. There is a delicate paradox here. If one gains wisdom only at the age of forty, one must retain the strength to put it to use. Most of us do not, however. This is Jōchō's warning.

31. Adversity

The following advice is simple:

A samurai who becomes tired or discouraged in times of misfortune is of no use. (Book Two)

One must not lose heart in misfortune.

32. Secret Love

The ultimate love I believe to be secret love. Once shared, love shrinks in stature. To pine away for love all one's years, to die of love without uttering the beloved's name, this is the true meaning of love. (Book One)

It is unusual to speak of the 'stature' of an emotion. The American authority on Japanese literature, Donald Keene, in a commentary on Chikamatsu's love suicides,[10] once wrote that when the lovers set out on their *michiyuki*, the final pilgrimage to death, the tone and brilliance of the language is heightened, and the lovers themselves seem to grow taller. Two people who until then had been ordinary citizens of the town, a pitiful man and woman entangled in family and financial problems, suddenly attain the gigantic proportions of a tragic hero and heroine.

Love today has become the romance of pygmies (small natives living in Africa). The stature of love has become insignificant, and undeclared love is rare. Love is losing its scope; lovers are losing the courage to surmount obstacles, the revolutionary passion to change social morality; love is losing its abstract meaning. In concrete terms, the lover loses the joy of having won his love and the sorrow of having failed to win her: he loses the wide spectrum of human emotion, the power to idealize the object of his affection. As a result, the object, too, is infinitely lessened in stature. Love is relative, and if the other person's stature is lessened one's own stature is equally lessened. Throughout Tokyo, pygmy romances are rampant today.

33. Epicureanism

When a novel called *Marius the Epicurean*, by the British writer Walter Pater, appeared in Japanese translation under the title *Marius the Hedonist*, this difficult philosophical novel became an unexpected best seller because readers were attracted by the title alone. Taking as his subject matter the spiritual development of a young aristocrat in Rome during the rise of Christianity, Pater wrote a poetic analysis of the philosophical principles of Epicurus (a Greek philosopher who advocated hedonism) in the tale of the youth's philosophical development leading to his conversion to Christianity. Epicurean philosophy is often referred to as hedonistic. In reality, however, it is only a hair's breadth away from stoicism. Suppose you have a date with a certain girl and spend the night at a hotel with her. The next morning, feeling somehow let down, you go to the earliest show at the movie theatre. What you feel then, barely able to suppress a yawn while watching a grade-B movie, is no longer hedonistic pleasure. Hedonism is keeping in one's heart the strict rules peculiar to hedonism and taking care never to overstep them. The philosophy of Epicurus rejects carnal hedonism, in which pleasure leads to disillusionment and satisfaction degenerates into spiritual blankness. Satisfaction is the enemy of pleasure and brings forth nothing but disillusion. So Epicurus, like the philosophers of the Cyrenaic School, considers pleasure as the highest principle of a happy and virtuous life. But the goal of pleasure is *ataraxia* (the tranquility of God; having denied all desires). He eliminates the fear of death, which might threaten this pleasure: 'While we live, death is irrelevant; when we are dead, we do not exist. There is no reason to fear death.' Here we find a link between the philosophy of Epicurus and the hedonism of Jōchō Yamamoto, for in his philosophy of death there clearly lurks such Epicurean stoicism.

In the last analysis the only thing that matters is the resolution of the moment. A samurai makes one resolution after another, until they add up to his whole life. Once he realizes this, he need never feel impatient, he need seek nothing beyond the moment. He merely lives his life concentrating on his resolution. However, people tend to forget this, and to imagine that something else of importance exists. Very few realize the truth. Learning to follow one's resolution without error cannot be accomplished before the passage of many years. But after one has reached that stage of enlightenment, even if one does not consciously think about it one's resolution will never change. If one perfects a single resolution, one will be seldom confused. This is loyalty to one's beliefs. (Book Two)

34. The Times

Here again *Hagakure* is clearly inconsistent. Lamenting as he does the decadence of his era and the degeneration of the young samurai, Jōchō is also a realistic observer of the flow of time, and he makes the penetrating observation that capriciously resisting the flow of time almost never produces desirable results.

The climate of an age is unalterable. That conditions are worsening steadily is proof that we have entered the last stage of the Law.[11] However, the season cannot always be spring or summer, nor can we have daylight forever. Therefore it is useless to try to make the present age like the good old days a hundred years ago. What is important is to make each era as good as it can be according to its nature. The error of people who are always nostalgic for the old ways lies in their failure to grasp this point. On the other hand, people who value only what is up to date and detest anything old-fashioned are superficial. (Book Two)

35. Samurai Valour I

Young men must be trained in military valour so that each has the confidence that he is the best and bravest warrior in all Japan. On the other hand, a young samurai must evaluate his discipline daily, and he must quickly discard any shortcoming he finds. Unless one divides up the subject of samurai valour in this way, one will never get anywhere. (Book Two)

36. Samurai Valour II

A samurai must take great pride in his military valour; he must have the supreme resolution to die a fanatic's death ... (Book Two)

37. Once Again, Nihilism

Jōchō's nihilism creates a world of extremes. Although Jōchō extols human energy and pure action, he sees as futile the final products.

I thought about it along the way, and it occurred to me that human beings are extraordinarily cleverly devised puppets. Though they are not dangling from strings, they can walk, jump, even speak – how skilfully they are made. But all the same, before the next Bon Festival[12] they may die and come back to visit us as spirits. What a futile existence! People always seem to forget this. (Book Two)

38. Cosmetics

I do not know how many times I have cited this passage. Sometimes one wakes up with a hangover and one's colour is bad. At such times one had better apply some rouge. The following passage, encouraging samurai to use cosmetics, is shocking to those with a stereotyped concept of the Way of the Samurai. It may remind such people of the effeminate youth who dress so fastidiously. Even during the Taishō Period [1913–25], a product called Pompeiian Cream was all the rage, and young men of the day made up their faces with this cosmetic.

But this is far from what Jōchō means by rouge. Men must be the colour of cherry blossoms, even in death. Before committing ritual suicide, it was customary to apply rouge to the cheeks in order not to lose life colour after death. Thus the morality of not being ashamed before one's enemy requires that one beautify one's appearance just before death, taking precautions to preserve the robustness of life.

How much more important it is while one is alive, in a society of externally oriented morality, to hide the dispirited face of a hungover samurai, even if it must be done by applying rouge. Here is a 'key point' [in English] at which Jōchō's externally oriented philosophy ties up with aesthetics. This is because aesthetic considerations are always external in nature. And just as the ancient Greeks associated aesthetics with ethics, morality in *Hagakure* is determined by aesthetics. What is beautiful must be strong, vivid, and brimming with energy. This is the first principle; the second is that what is moral must be beautiful. It does not mean taking great care over clothing and becoming effeminate, but rather it brings together beauty and ethical goals in the greatest possible tension. Rouge used to mask a hangover is directly related to make-up before ritual suicide.

One should always be equipped with rouge and powder. Sometimes it may happen when waking up with a hangover that one's colour is bad. At such times one should take out one's rouge and apply it. (Book Two)

39. How to Hold a Meeting

I understand that in China it was from ancient times the practice to hold a meeting only after having first persuaded each person expected to attend so that at the meeting a consensus would be reached. Here is a passage in which Jōchō recommends some political wisdom to the Japanese, who do not have a similar custom.

Whenever there is to be a consultation, first talk with each person involved and then assemble the people whose opinion you need to hear, and make your decision. Otherwise, there will inevitably be people who resent your decision. Also, when there is an important conference, you should secretly ask the advice of people who are not directly involved. Since they have no personal interest at stake, often they understand the proper solution. If you consult people involved in the issue, they are apt to advise you in a way that will benefit them. The point is that such advice is not very useful. (Book Two)

40. Shinto

It is thought that the ancient Shinto concept of defilement is in direct conflict with the Way of the Samurai. According to one theory, however, the water that purifies defilement in Shinto ritual has been replaced in *bushidō* by death. Shinto shuns pollution by contact with death or blood, but when a samurai enters the battlefield, corpses and blood inevitably accumulate all around him. In *The Jeweled Cord* [*Tamadasuki*], written by Atsutane Hirata (a scholar of national studies during the late Edo Period),[13] detailed regulations are cited for guarding against contamination, such as the proscription that in order to avoid defilement through contact with death one must sit outside the threshold of a room in which a body has been laid out for viewing, or: 'Pus and bleeding are forms of pollution; in the case of bleeding piles, nose bleeds, and so on, one should purify oneself by performing ablutions and make a pilgrimage to a shrine.' A samurai, however, could not always be completely faithful to such ancient Shinto precepts. It is a rather convincing argument that they replaced with death the water that purifies all these defilements.

However, Jōchō proposes no such compromise policy with respect to Shinto.

'If the gods are the sort to ignore my prayers simply because I have been defiled by blood, I am convinced there is nothing I can do about it, so I go ahead with my worship regardless of pollution.' Jōchō tries to be faithful to the Way of the Samurai by vigorously rejecting the Shinto taboos. Here the traditional Japanese idea of defilement is completely trampled underfoot before the desire for violent action.

Although they say the gods dislike contamination, I have my own opinion on the subject. I never neglect my daily worship.

Even when I get spattered with blood on the battlefield, or stumble over corpses underfoot as I fight, I believe in the effectiveness of praying to the gods for military success and long life. If the gods are the sort to ignore my prayers simply because I have been defiled by blood, I am convinced there is nothing I can do about it, so I go ahead with my worship regardless of pollution. (Book Two)

41. Epicureanism Again

As I have said before, there is one essential precept of the *Hagakure* philosophy that contradicts and reinforces at the same time the famous statement, 'I discovered that the Way of the Samurai is death.'

Human life lasts but an instant. One should spend it doing what one pleases. In this world fleeting as a dream, to live in misery doing only what one dislikes is foolishness. Since this may prove harmful if misinterpreted, it is a trade secret I have decided not to pass on to young people. I like to sleep. In response to conditions in the present world, I think I shall stay at home and sleep. (Book Two)

42. Tension

What follows is not unrelated to the preceding passage. If for the sake of moral goals a man always strives to live beautifully, and if he considers death as the ultimate standard of that beauty, then all his days must be a continuum of tension. Jōchō, for whom laziness is the supreme vice, discovered a reason for living in a daily life of unrelieved tension that never lets up even for an instant. This is struggle in the midst of daily routine; it is the occupation of a samurai.

One may measure the stature of a person's dignity on the basis of external impression. There is dignity in assiduity and effort. There is dignity in serenity. There is dignity in closeness of mouth. There is dignity in observing proper etiquette. There is dignity in behaving always with propriety. There is great dignity too in clenched teeth and flashing eyes. All these qualities are externally visible. The most important thing is to concentrate on them at all times and to be totally sincere in displaying them. (Book Two)

43. Dignity

In connection with the preceding passage, one might ask, What is dignity? Dignity is the outward manifestation of inviolable self-respect; it is what makes a man a man. It is the firm belief that one would rather die than be despised by others. And the expression of such an attitude in social conduct inevitably causes people to keep their distance. To an extent, Jōchō advises us to become the sort of people others do not approach easily.

It is true of the lord of a *han*, elder statesmen, and senior councillors that they must remain slightly aloof in order to achieve anything important. If one is constantly followed around by hangers-on, it is difficult to get things done. One should bear this in mind. (Book Two)

44. Egotism

'Egoism' [in English] is different from 'egotism' [in English]. If a man has self-respect, and if his guiding principles are high, then it no longer matters what he says or does. He refrains from speaking ill of others, yet he never makes it a special practice to praise them. The fiercely independent samurai is the ideal of *Hagakure*.

It is wrong to speak ill of others. It is equally unbecoming to give them praise. A samurai should know his own stature, pursue his discipline with diligence, and say as little as possible. (Book Two)

45. Effeminacy

According to my son-in-law Gonnojō, young men these days are becoming effeminate. This is an age in which people of pleasant disposition, cheerful people, people who do not cause ill feelings, gentle people, are thought to be virtuous, so that everything has become passive and strong resolution is no longer valued . . . (Book Two)

This is an age of 'pleasant men and plucky women'. Anywhere we look, there is certainly no lack of charming men. We are surrounded by the stereotype of the man who is gentle, loved by all, never abrasive. He brims with a compromising, harmonizing spirit, and at heart he is a cool opportunist. This is what *Hagakure* calls effeminacy. Beauty is not beauty for the sake of being loved. It is a beauty of strength, for the sake of appearances and to avoid losing face. When one tries to be beautiful in order to be loved, effeminacy begins. That is spiritual cosmetics. And in this day and age, when even bitter medicine is encased in a sugar coating, people will accept only what is palatable and easy to chew. The need for resistance to the currents of the age is the same now as then.

46. The Proper Attitude in Human Relations

Here Jōchō, who has elsewhere preached sincerity in human relations, emphasizes the necessity for self-respect in dealing with others. Both points come from Jōchō's relentlessly realistic observations on personal relations.

. . . As a general rule one should not visit people uninvited. True friends are few indeed. Even when one has been invited, the visit is often depressing . . . (Book Two)

47. Pride

The following passage needs no comment.

Someone once said, 'There are two kinds of pride, inner and outer. A samurai who does not have both inward and outward pride is of no use. Pride may be compared to the blade of a sword, which must be sharpened and then replaced in its scabbard. From time to time it is drawn and raised to the level of one's eyebrows, wiped clean, and then replaced in its scabbard. If a samurai's sword is always drawn and he is constantly brandishing the naked blade, people will find him unapproachable, and he will have no friends. If on the other hand the sword is never drawn, it will rust, the blade will become dull, and people will make light of him. (Book Two)

48. The Benefits of Time

Jōchō observes humanity with the cool detachment of a nihilist and a realist. But although he knows that human life is as fleeting as a dream, he knows too that human beings must continue to grow and mature whether they like it or not. Time naturally seeps into people and fosters something inside them. If a samurai is not confronted today with his final hour, if he cannot die today, he must continue living, unspared until tomorrow.

When Jōchō lived to the advanced age of sixty-one, he must have felt keenly the cruelty of time. From one point of view, whether you die at twenty or sixty life is the same ephemeral wisp. From another point of view, however, time beneficently bestowed on this survivor a cool and penetrating wisdom and knowledge of human life that one who dies at twenty will never know. This is what Jōchō called 'serving'. As I have explained before, Jōchō, whose only concern was to serve his daimyo well, continued to advocate his ever-practical philosophy without abandoning his nihilistic view of the ephemeral nature of being. He says, 'If only you take good care of your health, eventually you will fulfil your greatest desire and serve your daimyo well,' a remark most uncharacteristic of *Hagakure*. For Jōchō, taking care of one's physical condition means keeping in one's heart the resolution to die and taking care of oneself so that one may at any time fight in the best possible physical condition; it

means to be brimming with vital strength, always to preserve 100 per cent of one's energy. Carried this far, Jōchō's
philosophy of death changes into a philosophy of life, but at
the same time it reveals a still deeper nihilism.

Everyone occasionally fails at something important because
he has been impatient. If one thinks there is still plenty of time,
one's wishes are apt to be fulfilled more quickly. Let us simply
say one's time will come. Think for a moment what things will
be like fifteen years from now. Everything probably will have
changed. People have written what are called 'accounts of the
future', but these do not seem to predict anything strikingly
different from today. Of the valuable people in service now, in
ten years probably not a single one will survive. Probably only
about half even of today's young people will still be alive. The
world is gradually worsening: when we run out of gold, silver
becomes a treasure; and when the silver is gone, copper
becomes the treasure. With the passage of time, human abilities
decrease, and so if one really pulls oneself together and makes
an effort, in fifteen years' time one will become a valuable samurai. And yet, since fifteen years go by as quickly as a dream, if
only you take good care of your health, eventually you will fulfil
your great desire and serve your daimyo well. In an age of great
men it is difficult to make a name for oneself. When the world
at large is going to seed it is relatively easy to excel. (Book Two)

Notes

1. *Hagakure* literally means 'hidden among the leaves'.
2. Saigyō (1118–90). An itinerant priest-poet whose main theme
was the transience of life and beauty, his most common image being
the cherry blossom.
3. *Sanka wakashū*. Saigyō's private poetry collection. The com-
piler and date of compilation are unknown.
4. Saga Han. A daimyo domain (*han*) in north-western Kyushu,
now included in Saga Prefecture.
5. Bashō Matsuo (1644–94). The outstanding hermit-poet and
poetry master of the early Edo Period (1600–1868). Famous for
haiku and poetic travel diaries.

Monzaemon Chikamatsu (1653–1725). The outstanding dramatist of the period. Wrote plays for the kabuki and puppet (*bunraku*) theatres. Known for historical drama and domestic plays, most of which portray double suicides by illicit lovers caught in a bind between duty and passion.

Saikaku Ihara (1642–93). The outstanding writer of fiction. Famous for stories about the townspeople of Osaka, the merchants, and the pleasure quarters.

6. *Waka kokindenju*. The transmission from master to pupil of certain secret, arcane information pertaining to the 'true' meaning of words appearing in the *Kokinshū*, an early tenth-century Imperial anthology of court poetry. Receiving this was considered a great honour.

7. Sanenori Nishisanjō. A master of classical poetry. The Nishisanjō family were for generations scholars of classical literature.

8. Osaka has for hundreds of years been famous for the business acumen and sheer energy of its merchants. Many of the largest commercial companies even today originated as Osaka companies.

9. Yoshitsune Minamoto (1159–89). A great popular military hero, the subject of many fantastic legends. The younger brother of Yoritomo Minamoto, the first Kamakura shogun. Yoritomo turned against Yoshitsune and eventually caused his suicide after an heroic last stand.

10. Chikamatsu's love suicides. See note 6.

11. The latter days of the Law. According to Buddhist doctrine, after the death of the historical Buddha the world would pass through three progressively degenerate stages. The last of these, called Mappō in Japanese, the end of the Law, was to last ten thousand years, during which time the original teachings of the Buddha would cease to be heard.

12. Bon Festival. A festival traditionally celebrated on 15 July. Food is offered at graves and Buddhist altars, and entertainment is provided for the spirits of ancestors thought to return to earth for a visit at that time.

13. Atsutane Hirata (1776–1843). Scholar of National Studies during the late Edo Period. A student of Norinaga Motoori. Took National Learning in the direction of ultra-nationalism; asserted the supremacy of Shinto over other religions.

How to Read *Hagakure*

The Japanese Image of Death

I discovered that the Way of the Samurai is death. In a life or death crisis, simply settle it by choosing immediate death. (Book Two)

It was in the season of death, during the war, that *Hagakure* was read. At that time, a novel called *La Mort* by Paul Bourget (French writer and critic, 1852–1935) was read avidly, and *Hagakure* was greatly recommended as a book that could strengthen the determination of young men going off to war.

At present, if *Hagakure* is read at all, I do not know from what point of view it is approached. If there is still a reason for reading it, I can only guess that it is for considerations completely opposite to those during the war. Our enormous frustration at not being able to die is mounting fast. When all other demands have been satisfied, death becomes our only unsatisfied desire. And no matter how one may beautify death, it is beyond doubt that death exists and bears down on us little by little.

Young people long for death in the abstract, whereas it is true of men who have reached middle age that the more time they have on their hands the more time they spend worrying about cancer. And cancer is murder more cruel than any political authority would dare to commit.

The Japanese have always been a people grimly conscious of death beneath the surface of their daily lives. But the Japanese concept of death is straight and clear, and in that sense it is different from the loathsome, fearful death as seen by Westerners. The medieval European god of death (Father Time) holding a large scythe has never existed in the Japanese imagination. The Japanese image of death is different, too, from the image of death in a country like Mexico, in the obscure corners of whose modern cities still tower the Aztec and Toltec ruins, completely taken over by death, overgrown with luxuriant summer growth. Not that kind of rough, wild death, but an image of death beyond which there exists a spring of pure water, from which tiny streams are continuously pouring their pure waters into this world, has long enriched Japanese art.

Death According to *Hagakure* and Death for the Kamikaze Suicide Squadrons

We have learned many philosophies of life from the West. We could not be ultimately satisfied only with philosophies of life, however. Similarly, we were unable to assimilate Buddhist philosophy, with its stultifying concept of sin and karma, according to which one is born and reborn throughout eternity.

Death for Jōchō has the strange, clear, fresh brightness of blue sky between the clouds. In its modernized form, it coincides oddly enough with the image of the Kamikaze squadron, which has been called the most tragic form of attack used during the war. The suicide squadrons were called the most inhuman method of attack, and after the war the young men who had died in them were dishonoured. However, the spirit of those young men who for the sake of their country hurled themselves to certain death is closest in the long history of Japan to the clear ideal of action and death offered in *Hagakure*, though if one were to examine their motives individually, one would certainly find that they had their fears and their hardships. I suppose some people will say that the Kamikaze pilots, despite their high-sounding name, were forced to die. And certainly these youths not yet out of school were forced by the national authorities to proceed to their death against their will. Even if they went of their own will, they were rounded up into attack forces almost by coercion and sent to certain death. And this is certainly true.

There Is No Distinction Between Chosen Death and Obligatory Death

In that case is the death at which Jōchō is hinting exactly the opposite – death by choice? I do not think so. Jōchō begins by proposing death as a conduct one may choose, and he urges us to the decision to die. But beneath the surface of this man, who was forbidden to commit suicide at the death of his daimyo, there remained deep tidepools of nihilism after death receded and abandoned him. If a man is not perfectly free to choose death, he cannot be completely coerced into it. Even in the case of capital punishment, the extreme form of obligatory death, if the condemned tries to resist death spiritually, it ceases to be a simple obligatory death. Even death by a nuclear bomb, that overwhelming death by coercion, to the victims themselves was death by destiny. We are unable to come face to face with death until we are cornered between fate and our own choice. And to the final form of death there clings eternally the covert struggle between human choice and superhuman destiny. Sometimes it may appear that a man has died by his own choice. Suicide is an example. Sometimes a death may seem totally coerced. Death by bombing in an air raid is of this sort.

But even in suicide, seemingly the ultimate expression of free will, in the process leading to inevitable death, fate, over which one has no control, plays a part. And even in the case of a seemingly natural death, such as death from illness, it is by no means rare that in the process leading to that illness there is something which makes it seem almost as much a self-chosen death as suicide. The conditions for the decision to die that *Hagakure* seems to be encouraging are not always given to us in a bright and clear form. The enemy appears, one fights the enemy, and, given the choice between life and death, one makes the decision to die: These conditions are not always readily accorded one, not even in the days when there were no weapons more terrible than the Japanese sword. As proof, Jōchō himself lived on until the age of sixty-one.

In other words, no one has the right to say of *Hagakure* and the special suicide squadron that death for one is death by choice and death for the other is by coercion. The distinction can only be made in the cool, grim reality of an individual facing death; it is a question of the human spirit in the ultimate state of tension.

Can One Die for a Just Cause?

At this point, we must tackle the most difficult problem concerning death. Can righteous death, death chosen by us for the sake of a self-chosen righteous goal, can such a death in fact exist? Many young people today say they do not wish to die in an unjust war like the Vietnam war, but if they were required to die for a just national cause, or for the ideal of human salvation, they would go gladly to their deaths. This attitude is partly the fault of postwar education, especially the attitude that one shall not repeat the mistake of those who died for mistaken national objectives during the war and that from now on one shall die only for causes which one believes to be just.

But as long as human beings carry on their lives within the framework of a nation, can they really limit themselves to such righteous objectives? And even without taking the nation as a premise for existence, even when one lives as an individual transcending the nation, will one have the opportunity to choose to die for the sake of a just goal for humanity? Here must always arise a discrepancy between the absolute concept of death and the man-made, relativistic concept of righteousness. And the justness of the goals for which we die now – in one decade or several, or maybe one hundred or even two hundred years later – will perhaps be revised and overturned by history. The nit-picking and presumptuousness of human moral judgement *Hagakure* places in an entirely different category from death. Ultimately we cannot choose death. This is why Jōchō recommends death in a crisis of life or death. Certainly *Hagakure* does not say that this amounts to choosing death: We do not possess the standard for choosing to die. The fact that we are alive may mean that we have already been chosen for some purpose, and if life is not something we have chosen for ourselves, then maybe we are not ultimately free to die.

No Death Is in Vain

And what does it mean for a living being to confront death? According to *Hagakure*, what is important is purity of action. Jōchō affirms the height of passion and its power, and he also affirms any death thus arrived at. This is what he means when he says that calling a death in vain is the 'calculating *bushidō* of arrogant Osaka merchants'. Jōchō's most important pronouncement on death, 'I have discovered that the Way of the Samurai is death' cuts through with one stroke of the sword the Gordian knot, the adversary relationship between life and death.

Some say that to die without accomplishing one's mission is to die in vain, but this is the calculating *bushidō* (samurai ethic) of arrogant Osaka merchants. To make the correct choice in a fifty-fifty situation is nearly impossible.

Accomplishing one's mission, in modern terms, means to die righteously for a just cause, and *Hagakure* is saying that on the point of death one is by no means able to evaluate the justice of the cause.

'We would all prefer to live, and so it is quite natural in such a situation that one should find some excuse for living on.' A human being can always find some excuse. And human beings, simply by virtue of their being alive, must invent some sort of theory. *Hagakure* is simply expressing the relativistic position that rather than to live on as a coward having failed in one's mission, it is better to die. *Hagakure* by no means maintains that in dying one cannot fail to accomplish one's mission. Here is the nihilism of Jōchō Yamamoto, and here, too, is the ultimate idealism, born of his nihilism.

We tend to suffer from the illusion that we are capable of dying for a belief or a theory. What *Hagakure* is insisting is that even a merciless death, a futile death that bears neither flower nor fruit, has dignity as the death of a human being. If we value so highly the dignity of life, how can we not also value the dignity of death? No death may be called futile.

Appendix

Selected Words of Wisdom
from *Hagakure*

Introduction – Leisurely Talks in the Shadow of Night

The retainer of a daimyo must be well versed in the basic history and tradition of the domain. These days a retainer who studies intently is looked down upon. The essence of such study is to familiarize oneself with the origins of the daimyo house, and to engrave in one's memory how the house came to flourish through the trials and tribulations and the benevolence of our ancestors ... Katsushige, the first daimyo of Nabeshima, once said: '... Since these are peaceful times, the ways of the world are becoming flashy and extravagant. At this rate the martial arts will eventually fall into neglect, arrogance will prevail, one failure will follow another, those of high and low status alike will find themselves in straitened circumstances, there will be loss of face within the domain and without, and in the end the daimyo house will certainly fall to ruin. Looking around me at the people in the household, I see that the old men are dying and the youth are alert only to the trends of the times. Perhaps if I write some information by way of instruction for posterity and leave it to the daimyo house, young people may see it and through it gain at least some understanding of the essence of our domain's traditions.' Katsushige produced several written works, spending his whole life half buried in scraps of wastepaper. Of course, what concerns secret traditions I have no way of knowing, but the old samurai tell me that the military art of *kachikuchi* (the way to certain victory) was passed on from one generation of daimyo to the next by word of mouth. On his bookshelf Katsushige kept several important books of privileged information, and these were to be passed on from hand to hand. In addition it is said that he entered information in a notebook of elegant glossy paper about the customs and practices of the daimyo house and various organizations within the domain, including advice concerning official functions in connection with relations with the central government and detailed job descriptions of specific positions. His effort was a prodigious and invaluable one thanks to which the House has long prospered. With all due respect, one wishes that the present daimyo would bear in mind the trials and tribulations of the founder of the *han*, Naoshige, and the first daimyo, Katsushige, and would at least take a careful look at the books handed down to him. Since birth he has been surrounded by people who call him 'Young Master' and humour him, and he has grown up without knowing hardship, totally ignorant of our tradition, selfish and strong-willed. He never throws himself into his duties but instead is always trying something new for the sake of novelty. As a result inside the domain everything is going to seed. In times like these, clever men who really know nothing at all boast to each other of their great wisdom as they sit around thinking of something new and different to curry favour with the daimyo and intrude in *han* affairs. They do absolutely anything they please ... Having surveyed the situation, I determined to repay my own debt of gratitude to the Nabeshima House by being of some use in these degenerate times. If my efforts are warmly received, then all the more will I abandon selfish interest and devote my life to my domain, and even though I may be made a ronin or ordered to commit ritual suicide, I shall obey calmly, thinking that it is simply part of my samurai service. Even from retirement deep in the mountains, even from the grave, though I die and am reborn again and again, the determination to serve the Nabeshima House is the first resolution of a Nabeshima samurai and my reason for living. It is, I suppose, an unseemly attitude for one who has shaved his head and retired from the secular world, but I had never desired to attain buddhahood. Even if I were to die and be reborn again seven times, I neither expected nor wanted anything more than to be a Nabeshima samurai and to devote myself entirely to the *han*. In a word, all that is necessary for a Nabeshima samurai is that he have the strength of will to bear on his shoulders total responsibility for the ruling house of his *han*. We are all human beings. Why should one man be inferior to another? Skill and training are of no use unless one has great confidence in oneself. And if one does not use it for the peace and prosperity of the ruling house, training amounts to nothing. However, such resolution, like water boiling in a kettle, cools as easily as it was heated. Of course, there is a way to keep it from cooling. My methods consists of the four vows that follow: (1) Never fall behind in the Way of the Warrior. (2) Serve your lieged lord well. (3) Be filially pious. (4) Be deeply compassionate and help all human beings.

If every morning one prays to the gods and buddhas for help in carrying out these four vows, one's strength will double and there will be no back-sliding. Just like an inchworm, one will advance slowly. Even the gods and the buddhas make such vows.

The Chinese character *gen* (幻) can be read in Japanese as *maboroshi* and means 'illusion'. In Japanese, Indian magicians are called *genshutsushi* (幻出師), or 'illusionists'. Human beings in this life are like marionettes. That is why one uses the character *gen*, to suggest that free will is an illusion.

Hagakure: Book One

I Discovered that the Way of the Samurai is Death

I discovered that the Way of the Samurai is death. In a fifty-fifty life or death crisis, simply settle it by choosing immediate death. There is nothing complicated about it. Just brace yourself and proceed. Some say that to die without accomplishing one's mission is to die in vain, but this is the calculating, imitation samurai ethic of arrogant Osaka merchants. To make the correct choice in a fifty-fifty situation is nearly impossible. We would all prefer to live. And so it is quite natural in such a situation that one should find some excuse for living on. But one who chooses to go on living having failed in one's mission will be despised as a coward and a bungler. This is the precarious part. If one dies after having failed, it is a fanatic's death, death in vain. It is not, however, dishonourable. Such a death is in fact the Way of the Samurai. In order to be a perfect samurai, it is necessary to prepare oneself for death morning and evening day in and day out. When a samurai is constantly prepared for death, he has mastered the Way of the Samurai, and he may unerringly devote his life to the service of his lord.

Insight and Decision

Some people are born with the ability to call forth instantaneous wisdom whenever the occasion demands. Others however, must lie awake at night long afterwards, pounding their pillows in anguished concentration until they finally come up with a solution to the problem. But while such inborn differences in ability are inevitable to a certain extent, by adopting the Four Vows, anyone may develop hitherto undreamed-of wisdom. It might seem that no matter how limited one's abilities, no matter how difficult the problem, one ought to be able to find a solution if one thinks hard enough long enough, but as long as one bases one's reasoning on the 'self', one will simply be wily and not wise. Human beings are foolish, and it is difficult for them to lose the 'self'. Even so, when faced with a difficult situation, if one sets aside the specific problem for a moment, concentrates on the Four Vows and leaves the 'self', and then searches for a solution, one will not often miss.

Know the Limits of Your Abilities

Although we possess very little wisdom indeed, we tend to try to solve all our difficulties on the basis of it, with the unfortunate result that we become preoccupied with the self and turn our backs on the way of Heaven, and in the end our actions become evil. Indeed to an onlooker we must seem shabby, weak, narrow-minded, and totally ineffectual. When true wisdom seems unattainable on one's own strength, it is advisable to consult with those who are wiser. Someone who is not personally involved will be able to make a clear judgement uncomplicated by personal interest and will make the proper choice. Looking at a man who makes his decisions in such an admirable way, we know that he is sturdy, reliable, firmly rooted in reality. His wisdom, gathered through consultation with others, is like the roots of a great tree, numerous and thick. There are limits to the wisdom of one man, a lone sapling blown by the wind.

The Proper Way to Criticize Others

Reprimanding people and correcting their faults is important; it is actually an act of charity – the first requirement of samurai service. One must take pains to do it in the proper way. It is an easy matter to find strong points and shortcomings in another man's conduct; it is equally easy to criticize them. Most people seem to believe it a kindness to tell people things they do not want to hear, and if their criticisms are not taken to heart, well, then nothing more can be done. Such an approach is totally without merit. It produces results no better than if one had set out wilfully to insult and embarrass the man. It is simply a way of getting something off one's chest. Criticism must begin *after* one has discerned whether or not the person will accept it, *after* one has become his friend, shared his interests, and behaved in such a way as to earn his complete trust so that he will put faith in whatever one says. And then there is the matter of tact: one must devise the proper way to say it, and the proper moment – perhaps in a letter, perhaps on the way home from a pleasant gathering. One might start by describing one's own failures, and make him see what one is getting at without a word more than is necessary. First one praises his strengths, taking pains to encourage him and put him in the right mood, making him as receptive to one's words as a thirsty man to water. Then correct his faults. To criticize well is extremely difficult.

I know from personal experience that bad habits acquired over many years are not so easily broken. It seems to me that the properly charitable attitude is for all samurai in the service of the daimyo to be always in familiarity and friendship and to correct each other's faults the better to serve the daimyo together. By wilfully embarrassing someone, one accomplishes nothing – how could such tactics be effective?

How to Stifle a Yawn

To yawn in public is disrespectful. When you suddenly feel the urge to yawn, stroke your forehead upwards towards your scalp, and the yawn will subside. If that does not work, close your mouth and lick the inside of your lips – or else yawn discreetly into your sleeve or cover your mouth with your hand in order to be as inconspicuous as possible. The same policy applies to sneezes. If you do not attend carefully to such matters, you will look ridiculous. In addition, there are many other ways in which you must be careful to restrain yourself.

Plan Ahead

It is advisable always to make plans the evening before and make a note of the schedule. This is one way of staying a step ahead of other people. Whenever the daimyo was to make an appearance somewhere, the night before he always investigated the people who were to receive him at his destination and planned his words of greeting accordingly and the conversation to be exchanged. You should take a lesson from the daimyo and when you are to accompany someone on a journey or when you have been granted an audience with someone, you must first consider what kind of man your companion or host is. This is the way of harmony. It is also etiquette. When you receive an invitation from an important person, if you consider it a chore you will never be able to conduct yourself properly. You should go confident that a delightful time is in store for you. In general, except on business, it is better not to go where one has not been invited. Even if one has been invited, one cannot truly be called a proper guest unless one can be said to have behaved as a perfect guest should. In any case, it is essential to know beforehand what the affair is to be like and how one should behave. Most important of all is the drinking etiquette. How one sits is crucial. One must never allow the gathering to become tiresome, nor must it end early. It is never a good idea to overdo restraint when offered a meal; in fact, it may be discourteous. Refuse politely once or twice, and then if urged further go ahead and accept. This is also good policy when one happens to go somewhere and is unexpectedly asked to stay.

Investigate Everything Beforehand

In military science one speaks of the 'enlightened samurai' and the 'unenlightened samurai'. A samurai who has simply learned from direct experience how to act when confronted with difficult situations is not enlightened. A truly enlightened samurai investigates beforehand all possible situations and solutions so that he will be able to perform brilliantly when the time comes. Therefore, an enlightened samurai is one who settles every detail ahead of time. The unenlightened samurai may seem to muddle through a difficult situation, but his apparent success is merely his good fortune. It is truly an unenlightened samurai who does not study all eventualities ahead of time.

Fish Do Not Live in Clear Water

A certain person is constantly preaching strict austerity, but I disagree. As the proverb says, 'Fish do not live in clear water.' It is the seaweed that provides fish with a hiding place in which to grow safely to maturity. It is because one sometimes overlooks details and does not lend an ear to minor complaints that those in one's service are able to live in peace. An understanding of this point is essential when considering the character and deportment of others.

Approach a Task with Courage

When I asked Yasaburō for a sample of his calligraphy, he remarked, 'One should write boldly enough to cover the entire paper with a single character, with vigor enough to destroy the paper. Skill in calligraphy depends entirely on the energy and spirit with which it is executed. A samurai must proceed unflagging, never tiring or becoming dispirited, until the task is completed. That is all,' and he wrote the calligraphy.

Present-day 'Salarymen' Set Their Sights Too Low

Looking at young samurai in service these days, it seems to me they set their sights pitifully low. They have the furtive glance of pickpockets. Most of them are out for their own interests, or to display their cleverness, and even those who seem calm of heart are simply putting up a good front. That attitude will never do. Unless a samurai sets his sights on no less than offering up his life for his ruler, dying swiftly and becoming a spirit, unless he is constantly anxious about the welfare of his daimyo and reports to him immediately whenever he has disposed of a problem, his concern being always to strengthen the foundations of the realm, then he cannot be called a true samurai in the service of his lord. In that sense, daimyo and retainer must be of the same determination. Therefore, it is absolutely necessary to stand firm with a resolution so strong that not even the gods and buddhas may cause one to swerve from one's purpose.

Truly Virile Man Have Disappeared

I heard this from an acquaintance of mine. Apparently, a Doctor Kyōan once made the following statement: 'In medicine we distinguish between men and women by attributing to them the principles of yin and yang, and medical treatment originally differed accordingly. The pulse is also different. Over the past fifty years, however, the pulse of men has gradually become the same as that of women. Since noticing this phenomenon, I have considered it proper to treat eye diseases of male patients with the method normally appropriate to the pulse of women patients. When I try applying to my male patients the cures appropriate to men, they produce no effect whatever. The world is indeed entering a degenerate stage; men are losing their virility and are becoming just like women. This is an unshakeable truth I have learned from first-hand experience. I have decided to keep it a secret from the world at large.' When with this story in mind I look around me at the men of today, I often think to myself, 'Aha. There goes an example of a female pulse.' Almost never do I see what I call a true man. And for that very reason, these days it is possible to excel and reach a position of importance with a modicum of effort.

As proof that today men are becoming cowardly weaklings even so, consider the fact that few are those who have had the experience of beheading a criminal with his hands tied behind his back, and when asked to perform the role of second in a ritual suicide, most men now consider it intelligent to come up with an ingenious excuse. Until forty or fifty years ago, having been wounded in combat was a mark of virility, and an unscarred thigh was so blatant a sign of inexperience or cowardice that a man would not dare expose it in public, preferring to inflict a wound on himself to create a scar if necessary. Men were expected to be hot-blooded and impetuous. Today, however, impetuosity is considered idiotic, and men with clever tongues use them to dispatch their responsibilities without lifting a finger. I should like young people to consider this point well.

Human Beings Are Like Marionettes

The Chinese character *gen* (幻) can be read in Japanese as *maboroshi* and means 'illusion'. In Japanese, Indian magicians are called *genshutsushi* (幻出師), or 'illusionists'. Human beings in this life are like marionettes. That is why one uses the character *gen*, to suggest the 'illusion' of free will.

'The Advantage Is to the Onlooker'

To hate evil and live one's life in rightousness is exceedingly difficult. Surprisingly enough, many errors arise from believing that it is essential to be strictly logical and to value righteousness above all else. There is a way more lofty than righteousness, but discovering it is no easy matter and requires wisdom of the highest order. Compared to this Way, logical principles are insignificant indeed. What one has not experienced first-hand one cannot know. And yet, there is a means of learning the truth even though one has not been able to discern it for oneself. The way lies in talking with other people. It is often true that even a person who has not yet perfected himself may be able to give directions to others. The principle involved is similar to what in *go* is called 'The advantage is to the onlooker.' One speaks of 'learning one's faults through contemplation', but this too is best done by talking with others. The reason is that when one learns by listening to what others have to say and by reading books, one transcends the limitations of one's own powers of discernment and follows the teachings of the ancients.

There Is Always Room for Improvement

I heave heard that a certain master swordsman, having reached old age, made the following statement:

'A samurai's training lasts a lifetime, and there is a proper order to it. At the lowest level of training, even though you practise, you do not seem to improve, you know you are unskilful, and you believe the same of others. At this point, needless to say, you are of no use in the service of the daimyo. At the middle level you are still of no real use, but you are aware of your deficiencies, and you begin to recognize the shortcomings of others. When a samurai attains the highest level, he is able to dispose of any situation on the basis of his own wisdom so that he no longer need follow the teachings of others; he gains confidence in his abilities, rejoices in being praised, and laments the failings of others. Such a samurai, may we well say, is useful in the service of the daimyo. Even above this level, there are those whose facial expressions never reveal what they are thinking, nor do they make an exhibition of their skill – in fact, they feign ignorance and incompetence. What is more, they respect the skill of others. In most cases I suppose this is the best that can be aspired to.

'But on a still higher level there is an extreme realm that transcends the skill of ordinary mortals. One who penetrates

deep into the Way of this realm realizes that there is no end
to his training, and that the time will never come when he
may be satisfied with his labours. Therefore, a samurai must
know his shortcomings well and spend his life in training
without ever feeling he has done enough. Of course he must
never be over-confident, but neither should he feel inferior
to others.'

Yagyū, a teacher of *kendō* to the Tokugawa shoguns, is
quoted as having said, 'I do not know how to excel others.
All I know is how to excel myself.' Saying to himself,
'Today I am better than I was yesterday, tomorrow I will be
still better,' a true samurai lives out his days in constant
effort to improve. That is what training is, a process without
end.

One Should Take Important Considerations Lightly

Among the public proclamations of Lord Naoshige is the
following: 'One should take important considerations
lightly.' A commentary by Ittei Ishida (Confucian scholar of
Saga Han, and Jōchō Yamamoto's teacher) explains, 'Small
matters should be taken seriously.' Truly important problems are few; they occur probably no more than twice or
thrice in a lifetime. Everyday reflection will tell you this.
Therefore, it is necessary to plan ahead what to do in case of
a crisis, and then when the time comes, to remember the
plan and dispose of the problem accordingly. Without daily
preparation, when faced with a difficult situation one may be
unable to reach a quick decision, with disastrous results.
Therefore, may we not say that daily resolution upon a certain course of action is the principle behind the statement,
'One should take important considerations lightly'?

*When One Cannot Decide Whether to Live or Die, It Is
Better to Die*

The famous samurai retainer Kiranosuke Shida has said,

'If your name means nothing to the world whether you live or die, it is better to live.' Shida is a formidable samurai, and young people have misinterpreted these words of his said in jest and have mistakenly thought he was advocating dishonourable conduct. In a postscript, he adds: 'When in doubt whether to eat or not eat, it is better to refrain. When one cannot decide whether to live or die, it is better to die.'

A Man Who Never Errs Is Not to Be Trusted

Once in the course of a debate over the promotion of a certain man, it came out that the man in question had once been a heavy drinker, and everyone then felt inclined to deny him his promotion. Someone present, however, insisted: 'If we completely abandon a man because he has committed a single error, we will never produce a truly superior personage. A man who has once erred deeply regrets his mistake, conducts himself with propriety and self-control, and turns out to be remarkably useful in service. Promote this man.' Whereupon someone else said, 'Will you assume responsibility for the outcome?' When he assured them that he would, everyone pressed him for a reason. He replied, 'I accept full responsibility for him because he is a man who has once erred. A man who has never made a mistake is not to be trusted.' The man got his promotion after all.

Instead of Victory, Concentrate on Dying

A man once was disgraced because he failed to revenge himself for a wrong done him. The true way to take revenge is to march right into the enemy camp and fight until you are cut down. If a samurai throws himself into the fray, he will not end in disgrace. It is because one hopes to succeed that one does not measure up. While one is thinking that one is outnumbered and in for trouble, time passes; eventually, one may decide to forget the whole thing. Even though the enemy may number in the scores, if one stands one's ground determined to run them all through single-handed, the quarrel will soon be settled. In fact, things will probably go well. Even in the case of the Forty-seven Ronin of the Asano house, who finally attacked Kira at night to revenge the death of their lieged lord, they missed their mark originally in not committing ritual suicide together at Sengakuji immediately. As it happened, they took their time about revenging the death of their lord, and if Kira himself had fallen ill and died before they could put their plan into practice, they would have lost the chance forever ...

As a rule, I do not criticize the conduct of others, but since we are investigating the Way of the Samurai, I feel I should say this. If one does not consider closely all contingencies beforehand, when the time comes one will not be able to reach a sound conclusion, with the result that one will usually bring dishonour on oneself.

Learning from what others tell you, and trying to discern the essence of things, is preparation for forming your resolution before the crisis occurs. Among other things, the Way of the Samurai requires that he realize that something may occur at any moment to test the depth of his resolution, and day and night he must sort out his thoughts and prepare a line of action. Depending on the circumstances, he may win or lose. But avoiding dishonour is quite a separate consideration from winning or losing. To avoid dishonour he must die. But if the first time things do not proceed as he would wish, he must try again. For this he needs no special wisdom or skill. The stubborn samurai thinks not of victory or defeat but merely fights insanely to the death. It is only then that the realization comes.

Do Not Form Fixed Opinions

It is wrong to have strong personal convictions. If through

diligence and concentration of mind a samurai acquires fixed opinions, he is apt to reach the hasty conclusion that he has already attained an acceptable level of performance; this is most inadvisable. A samurai must pile diligence upon diligence, attaining first total mastery over the basic principles and skills, then continuing his training so that basic skills will reach fruition. A samurai must never relax but pursue his training throughout his life. To think that one may relax one's discipline simply because one has made some personal discoveries is the height of foolishness. A samurai must always think, 'On this and that point I am still far from perfection,' and spend his whole life in training, searching assiduously for the true Way. It is in the process of such training only that one may find the Way.

Daily Resolution

Until fifty or sixty years ago, samurai performed their ablutions every morning, shaved their heads, and perfumed their topknots. Then they cut their fingernails and toenails, filed them with pumice, and finally buffed them with *kogane* herb. They were never lazy about such matters but took great care to be well groomed. Then a samurai took a look at his long and short swords to make sure that they were not rusting, wiped off the dust, and polished them. Taking such pains over one's appearance may seem foppish, but the custom did not arise from a taste for elegance or romance. One may be run through at any moment in vigorous battle; to die having neglected one's personal grooming is to reveal a general sloppiness of habit, and to be despised and mocked by the enemy. So in youth as in old age samurai took pains to look their best. Such fastidiousness may seem time-consuming and more trouble than it is worth, but it is what the Way of the Samurai is all about. Actually, it takes little trouble or time. If, always prepared to die, a samurai begins to think of himself as already dead, if he is diligent in serving his lord and perfects himself in the military arts, surely he will never come to shame; but if a samurai spends his days selfishly doing exactly as he pleases, in a crisis he will bring dishonour upon himself. Having done so, he will not even be aware of his shame, and imagining that as long as he is secure and happy nothing else matters, he will disport himself unspeakably – a thoroughly lamentable development.

A samurai who is not prepared to die at any moment will inevitably die an unbecoming death. But a samurai who lives his life in constant preparation for death – how can he conduct himself in a despicable manner? One should reflect well on this point and behave accordingly. Times have changed in the last thirty years. Now when young samurai get together they talk of money, of profit and loss, how to run a household efficiently, how to judge the value of clothing, and they exchange stories about sex. If any other topic is mentioned, the atmosphere is spoiled and everyone present feels vaguely uncomfortable. What a distressing pass things have come to! It used to be that until the age of twenty or thirty a young man never thought a mean or worldly thought, and so of course he never spoke of such things. And if in their presence older men by accident should let such a remark escape their lips, young men felt as afflicted by it as if they had been physically wounded. Apparently, the new trend has arisen because the modern age has come to value luxury and ostentation. Money alone has come to assume great importance. Certainly if young men did not have luxurious tastes inappropriate to their stations, this mistaken attitude would disappear.

On the other hand, to praise as resourceful young people who are economical and frugal is quite despicable. Frugality inevitably amounts to lacking a sense of *giri*, or personal and social obligations. Need I add that a samurai who forgets his obligations to others is mean, base, and ignoble?

Every Human Being Has Much to Learn

According to the Confucian scholar Ittei Ishida, even a clumsy writer can learn to write a passable hand if he follows scrupulously and diligently a good copybook. The same may be said of samurai service. If one takes a good samurai as one's model, one will probably turn out rather well. These days there are unfortunately no samurai around worthy of total imitation, and so one must create in the mind's eye a suitable model for emulation. The way to create such a model is to think who among one's acquaintances knows how to observe etiquette, propriety, and ceremony; who has the most courage; who is the most eloquent; who is morally beyond reproach; who has the most integrity; who can make up his mind quickly in a crisis, and then to imagine a composite of all these people. The result will be an excellent model quite worthy of imitation.

It is true of any art that the master's strong points are difficult to learn but his weaknesses are easily acquired by his students – and of course such weak points are of no use at all. There are people who know etiquette but are lacking in integrity. When one attempts to learn from such a person, one tends to ignore the etiquette and imitate only the lack of integrity. When one learns to recognize the strong points of others, anyone may become one's model, anyone may be one's teacher.

How to Behave at a Drinking Party

Many men have failed in life as a result of overdrinking. This is exceedingly unfortunate. One must know one's capacity for drink, and it is advisable never to drink more. Even so, one occasionally miscalculates. A samurai must never relax his guard when drinking, so that if ever something unexpected should occur he would be able to deal with it appropriately. Banquets where alcohol is served are like the 'open air', and there are many observing eyes. One must be careful.

Never Lose Heart

When calling on a friend who has met with a personal disaster, what one says to him by way of encouragement is extremely important. He will be able to read one's real motives in these words. A true samurai must never seem to flag or lose heart. He must push on courageously as though sure to come out on top. Otherwise he is utterly useless. Here is the secret of encouraging a friend in trouble.

Lesson for a Rainy Day

There is something called the 'rainstorm attitude'. When caught in a sudden shower, one may determine not to get drenched, running as fast as one can or trying to thread one's way under the eaves of houses along the way – but one gets wet none the less. If from the outset one is mentally prepared to get wet, one is not in the least discomfited when it actually happens. Such an attitude is beneficial in all situations.

A Samurai Must Be Confident of His Surpassing Merit

The Golden Mean is greatly valued, but when it comes to the martial arts, even in daily practice a samurai must constantly feel that his skill surpasses that of everyone else. In archery we have target practice. If one aims directly at the guidelines on the target, however, the arrow will tend to drift to the right and upward. The solution is to aim low and to the left. Then the arrow will hit its mark.

A samurai whose object is to excel on the battlefield, surpassing men of great military prowess, a samurai who spends his days and nights devising ways to capture a strong enemy, is the personification of samurai valour, vigorous and indomitable. So say the brave old warriors' tales. In daily life, too, such must be one's resolution.

Initial Victory Is Victory Once and for All

In his old age Tetsuzan once made the following remark: 'I used to think that actual hand to hand combat differs from *sumō* wrestling in that it does not matter if you are floored early on, as long as you win in the end. But recently I have changed my mind. If a judge were to separate you at the point when you were on the ground, you would be declared the loser. To win from the beginning is to be the constant victor.'

The Education of Children

There is an established formula for raising a samurai child. In infancy his courage is stimulated, and no one must ever threaten or deceive him. If even as a child he suffers from anxiety or fears, the defect will be a scar he carries to his grave. A child should not be allowed to become frightened of thunder through the oversight of his parents, or forbidden to go into the dark, and it is bad policy to tell him frightening stories to keep him quiet when he cries.

On the other hand, if he is scolded too severely as a child, he will grow into a shy, introverted adult. In any event, one must take care that he does not acquire bad character traits. Once he has picked up an unfortunate trait, you will not rid him of it no matter how you lecture him. In speech and in etiquette he should be made to reach a general understanding of propriety, and he should never know vulgar desires. All other points are less important, since most normal, healthy children will grow up anyway regardless of their upbringing. It is of course true that children of a disharmonious marriage will be lacking in filial piety. Even the birds and beasts are influenced by what they see and hear from the moment they are born; one must be exceedingly careful about a child's environment. Sometimes things go badly between father and son because of a mother's foolishness. If a mother dotes unreasonably on her child and invariably takes the child's side when the father tries to scold him, she is forming a conspiracy with the child, which causes further friction between father and son. Conspiring with the child against the father apparently stems from a woman's natural shallowness of purpose and her calculation that by winning the favour of her son early in life she will ensure her well-being in years to come.

Artistic Accomplishments Lead to Personal Ruin

That an artistic accomplishment will help one earn a living is true only of samurai from other domains. For samurai of this ruling house, such accomplishments lead to debasement of status. Anyone who is especially skilled in a particular art is a technician, not a samurai. If a certain person, who shall remain nameless, wants to be considered a samurai, he must realize that any artistic accomplishment is a detriment to his samurai stature. Only when he realizes that this is so will all sorts of accomplishments in fact become useful to him. He should keep this point in mind.

Action Is Better Than Anticipation

Somebody or other once remarked: 'It is generally thought that nothing is harder than being a ronin, and when that fate befalls a man he immediately loses heart and utterly gives up. Actually, being a ronin was quite different from what I had imagined and not nearly so bad. In fact, I would like to be a ronin again for a while.' I agree with him. The same thing may be said about dying: If day in and day out a samurai rehearses death in his mind, when the times comes, he will be able to die calmly. Since disasters are never so formidable as in anticipation, it is utter foolishness to spend time worrying about them in advance. One had better resign oneself from the outset that the final destination of a samurai in the service of his lord is becoming a ronin or committing *seppuku*.

To Test a Person's True Feelings, Fall Ill

It is said, 'If you want to see into the heart of a friend, fall ill.' A person who is friendly to you in good times and turns his back on you like a stranger in times of illness or misfortune is a coward. It is most important when someone has met with ill-fortune, to stand by him, to visit him, and to take him what he needs. A samurai must never as long as he lives permit himself to be cut off from those to whom he is spiritually indebted. Here is a standard for evaluating a man's true feelings. But most of the time we turn to others for help in times of trouble and forget them entirely when the crisis has passed.

Worldly Success Is Simply a Matter of Fate

The goodness or evil of a man's character is not reflected in worldly success or failure. Prosperity and decline are, after all, the workings of nature, whereas good and evil are a question of human evaluation. Even so, for didactic purposes it is convenient to talk as though success or failure in the world were the direct result of a good or bad character.

The Proper Time to Fire a Servant

Zenjin'emon Yamamoto (Jōchō's father), when one of his servants committed an impropriety, would continue to keep him in his service for the rest of the year as though nothing had happened and then calmly give him his leave just before the new year.

A Man Who Looks Intelligent Will Never Succeed

In order to perfect his looks and his bearing, a samurai

should make a habit of correcting them by looking in the mirror. When I reached the age of thirteen I bound my hair into the traditional topknot, but then I remained secluded at home for about a year. I did this because everyone was saying, 'He has such a clever face that he is sure to wind up a failure. What the daimyo dislikes above all else is a person who looks intelligent.' So, determining to correct my facial expressions, I looked in the mirror day in and day out. After a year had passed and I reappeared, everyone remarked that I looked somehow not very healthy, and I thought to myself, this is what samurai service is all about. There is something that makes one hesitate to trust a man who shows his intelligence in his face. If a man's bearing lacks a sense of calm dignity and serenity, one cannot call it handsome. A reverent yet stern, self-collected appearance is ideal.

An Official Investigator Must Be Hard on His Superiors

Unless an official investigator [*metsuke*] is in a position to see the whole picture, he will do harm rather than good. The reason we have *metsuke* is to preserve law and order in the domain. The daimyo cannot all by himself keep track of what is going on in every corner of the land. The main job of the *metsuke* is to learn all he can about the conduct of the daimyo, the scruples of his elder statesmen, the vices and virtues of civil administration, public opinion, and the wealth and happiness of the people. Therefore, the *metsuke* were originally intended to be strict in surveying their superiors. And yet, today the *metsuke* spy out misbehaviour among the people, with the result that vice is rampant and they do harm rather than good. While it is true that there are few models of perfection among the people, their petty vices do no serious harm to that state. Moreover, the official in charge of investigating the truth or falsehood of a charge should actually hope that the testimony of the accused will prove true and that he will be spared punishment. Such an attitude too in the end will be to the advantage of the daimyo house.

One Must Not Calculate Everything on the Basis of Loss or Gain

A calculating man is a coward. I say this because calculations all have to do with profit and loss, and such a person is therefore constantly preoccupied with profit and loss. To die is a loss, to live a gain, and so one decides not to die. Therefore, one is a coward. Similarly, a man of education camouflages with his intellect and eloquence the cowardice or greed that is his true nature. Many people do not realize this.

Do Everything as though to the Death

Lord Naoshige said, 'The Way of the Samurai is a mania for death. Sometimes ten men cannot topple a man with such conviction.' One cannot accomplish feats of greatness in a normal frame of mind. One must turn fanatic and develop a mania for dying. By the time one develops powers of discernment, it is already too late to put them into effect. In the Way of the Samurai loyalty and filial piety are superfluous; all one needs is a mania for death. Within that attitude loyalty and filial piety will come to reside.

Hardship Is Cause for Rejoicing

It is not enough simply to avoid feeling discouraged in the face of hardship. When disaster befalls a samurai, he must rejoice and leap at the chance to proceed with energy and courage. Well might one say that such an attitude transcends mere resignation. 'When the water is high the boat rises.'

If the Master Is Human, I am a Human Being Too

It is pusillanimous to think after having heard of the feats of a master that one will never be his equal no matter how hard one tries. One must exert oneself, thinking, I am just as much a man as the master; why should I be inferior to him? Once a samurai sets himself to the challenge, he has already entered the way to improvement. Ittei Ishida has said, 'A man who is recognized as a sage gains that reputation because he began his pursuit of knowledge at a young age. It is not that he suddenly became a sage by hard training later in life.' In other words, at the time one first makes a resolution to achieve excellence one may experience true enlightenment.

A Samurai Never Relaxes His Guard

A samurai must be careful in all matters, and he must strictly avoid even minor failures. Sometimes a samurai does not watch his tongue and inadvertently makes a remark such as, 'I am a coward', 'If that happens, let's run for our lives', 'How terrifying', or 'Ouch'. Such words must never pass one's lips, not in jest, nor in fun, nor asleep, nor by accident, not in any context whatsoever. A perceptive person hearing such a remark will discern one's true nature. One must always be on one's guard.

Make Up Your Mind Within the Space of Seven Breaths

There is an old saying, 'Make up your mind within the space of seven breaths.' Lord Takanobu Ryūzōji once remarked, 'If one hesitates too long over a decision, one falls asleep.' Lord Naoshige said, 'When one proceeds in a leisurely fashion, seven out of ten actions turn out wrong.' It is extremely hard to make decisions when one is flustered. But if without worrying over minor issues one approaches the problem with a razor-sharp mind, one will always reach a decision within the space of seven breaths. Consider the problem calmly and with simple determination.

People Who Are Liked, and Those Who Are Disliked

A man with a little knowledge soon becomes arrogant and delights in being called a man of ability. Such people, who boast that they are too good for the modern age, who think no one is more talented than they, will inevitably be punished by Heaven.

No matter how great his ability, a man who is not liked is of no use at all. One who works hard, who likes his job, and who is extremely humble, who rather enjoys being in a subordinate position with respect to his equals, will be well liked.

One Must Not Win Fame and Fortune Too Early in Life

If one advances in the world as a young man, one will not be effective in the service of one's daimyo. No matter how clever the samurai may be by birth, his abilities are not fully developed when he is young and he will not be sufficiently accepted by others. When he has reached the age of fifty, he must gradually finish his preparation. Behaving in such a way that people believe his entering into public life is if anything slower than it should be, is actually the true way to commit himself to service. And even though he may ruin his fortunes, a man with the proper will has not done it by attempting wrongful gains to himself, and so he will recover it in time.

Stumble and Fall Seven Times, Bounce Back Eight

For a samurai to lose control over himself when he becomes a ronin or meets with a similar misfortune is the height of foolishness. Retainers in Lord Katsushige's day had a favourite saying: 'If you have not been seven times a ronin you cannot call yourself a true samurai. Stumble and fall seven times, bounce back eight times.' Apparently Hyōgo Naritomi, for one, was seven times a ronin. A samurai in the service of the daimyo must conceive of himself as a self-righting doll that bounces back no matter how many times you knock it down. In fact, it is a good idea for the daimyo to try giving retainers their liberty to test their spiritual strength.

Praise the Rank and File

In a poem about Yoshitsune is the following statement: 'A general must speak often to the rank and file.' The people who serve in one's household, similarly, will be ready to devote their lives to one's service willingly if, not merely in extraordinary circumstances but also on a regular basis, one offers them such personal comments as, 'How well you have served me,' 'You must take the greatest care on this point,' 'Now here is a hard worker.' Such remarks are all-important.

If You Wish To Excel, Invite Criticism from Others

If you wish to excel, the best way to do so is to ask the opinions of others and seek their criticism. Most people try to get by on the basis of their own judgement, and as a result they never make significant progress.

Once a man consulted another concerning a document he had prepared for the government office. The other man was far more skilled at composition than the first and was able to offer valuable suggestions. A man who seeks criticism from others is already superior to most.

If You Chase Two Rabbits, You Will Miss Them Both

It is wong to set one's mind on two things at once. One must devote all one's energy to the Way of the Samurai; one must seek for nothing more. The same principle applies to the character for 'Way' (道). However, one who has studied Confucianism or Buddhism may feel that the Way of the Samurai is an unreasonable 'Way'. Only if you study all the various 'Ways' will you eventually become able to understand what is truly reasonable.

Choose Your Words Carefully

The first thing a samurai says on any occasion is extremely important. He displays with this one remark all the valour of the samurai. In times of peace it is language that manifests valour. Even in times of chaos and destruction, great bravery may be revealed in a single word. One might say that this one word is a flower of the heart.

Never a Word of Weakness

Even in casual conversation, a samurai must never complain. He must constantly be on guard lest he should let slip a word of weakness. From a slight remark uttered inadvertently, one's true nature may be guessed.

A Man of Special Artistic Accomplishment Is Useless

A man who earns a reputation for being skilled at a technical art is idiotic. Because of his foolishness in concentrating his energies on one thing, he has become good at it by refusing to think of anything else. Such a person is of no use at all.

Be Especially Humble After the Age of Thirty

Many people give advice, but those who receive it gratefully are few. Still rarer are those who follow such advice. Once a man passes the age of thirty, there is no one to advise him. When advice ceases to reach him, he becomes wilful and selfish. For the rest of his life he adds impropriety to foolishness, until he is beyond redemption. Therefore, it is absolutely necessary to find someone who knows what is right, to become well acquainted with him, and to receive his instruction.

Set Your Sights on Honour and Wealth

A samurai who has no interest in wealth or honour usually ends up a petty human being, slandering others. Such a man is vain and useless and in the end proves inferior to a man who is ambitious for wealth and fame. He is of no immediate practical use.

Always Behave with the Reserve Appropriate to a First Meeting

When people live together in harmony and agreement, following the natural laws of Heaven and earth, their existence is peaceful and secure. A samurai whose heart is not harmonious and who does not have a friendly and flexible spirit is not a faithful retainer no matter how splendid his rhetoric. One may be getting along badly with a friend, but showing displeasure when one happens to meet him, or making twisted, sarcastic remarks, arises from the foolishness of a narrow mind. One should plan ahead and treat him thoughtfully, and even if one does not really mean it, and though it may be disagreeable, one should greet him pleasantly no matter how many times one may chance to meet.

Even though one makes such efforts, however, in this fleeting, unpredictable world one may well end up being disliked. This is unavoidable. One must not behave in a shallow way calculated to win favour. Such a man is thoroughly disgraceful because he never thinks of anything but personal interest. If one puts the other person before oneself, and without jealousy or competitiveness behaves according to etiquette, if one humbly thinks of the other person's interests even to one's personal disadvantage, each meeting will be as the first, and the relationship will never degenerate. The same may be said of conducting a marriage ceremony. If one allows oneself to relax as one gets used to the proceedings, one is sure to slip up towards the end.

If you continue to associate with a friend modestly and with propriety as though you were meeting for the first time though you have actually become quite familiar, you certainly will never quarrel.

True Love Comes Once in a Lifetime

The following is a remark made by a man called Shikibu: 'A samurai often has a homosexual experience in his youth that becomes a source of shame all his life.' This sort of thing is dangerous if he does not approach it with the proper attitude, but there is no one to instruct him in the matter. Therefore, I have decided to outline the proper conduct.

Even in homosexual love, 'a faithful wife never remarries'. You must have only one true love in your entire life; otherwise, you are no better than a male prostitute or a loose woman. Such conduct brings disgrace on a samurai. Saikaku put it well when he said, 'A youth without a sworn love is like a maiden without a betrothed: People cannot easily resist approaching them, though half in jest.'

When the other man is your senior, it is advisable to spend about five years getting to know each other, and when you finally understand the depth of the other's emotion, you should take the initiative and ask for a pledge. If it is to be a relationship in which each would give his life for the other, you must be perfectly aware of each other's innermost feelings. If someone else is pressing his attentions on you, you should shake him off abruptly, saying, 'Your overtures are offensive to me.' If he asks why, you answer, 'That is something I must not divulge as long as I live.' If he continues to press, you should get angry and cut him down on the spot. When the other man is younger, you must search out his innermost heart just as in the other case. If you stake your very life on the outcome, in five or six years your wishes may come true.

Of course you must not straddle the two Ways – love for men and love for women. Even while you are in love with a man, you must concentrate your energies on the Way of the Warrior. Then homosexual love goes very well with the Way of the Warrior.

Abandon Wisdom and Judgement

Until the age of forty a samurai should not be carried away by wisdom or judgement but should depend on ability and strength. The stronger he is, the better. It depends on the individual and his status in life, but even after forty a samurai carries little weight without strength of character.

Hagakure: Book Two

Pride may be compared to the blade of a samurai's sword . . . If the sword is never drawn, it will rust, the blade will become dull, and people will make light of him. (Book Two)

It Is Better To Know Hardship When Young

When I asked what a samurai in the service of the daimyo must never do, I was given the following answer: A samurai must never drink too much, be overconfident, or indulge in luxury. In time of misfortune these weaknesses are of no consequence whatever. But as soon as the situation begins to improve and life begins to get easier, these three faults are apt to prove fatal. Look at the careers of people you know. As soon as they begin to succeed, they are apt to be extraordinarily pleased with themselves, to become arrogant and indulge in inexcusable luxury, in the most unbecoming way. Therefore anyone who has never known suffering has not fully established his character. It is better to know hardship when young. A samurai who becomes tired or discouraged in times of misfortune is of no use.

The Ultimate Love Is Secret Love

The other day I was talking to a group of people, and I told them that the ultimate love I believe to be secret love. Once shared, love shrinks in stature. To pine away for love all one's years, to die of love without uttering the beloved's name, this is the true meaning of love. A poem tells us:

> I shall die for my love
> Know the truth only in the smoke that remains –
> My lover's name kept secret to the end.

The kind of love this poem describes is the most elegant kind of love. Once when I made this remark, apparently four or five people present, impressed by the poem, took up the line, 'Know the truth only in the smoke that remains,' and coined the phrase 'lovers in smoke'.

First Divine the Temperament of the Person You Are Talking to

When you are talking with someone, you should quickly divine his temperament and gauge your attitude towards him according to the situation. For example, when dealing with an argumentative snob, speak as humbly as possible so as not to offend him, all the while destroying his argument on the basis of the logical foundation that he himself has laid, and doing so in such a way that he is left with no resentment or dissatisfaction. This is the role of intuition and the importance of rhetoric . . .

Nice Guys Are Failures

Nice guys finish last. Human beings must be overflowing with vitality.

Training One's Superiors

With an even-tempered, cheerful lord, one must do one's best to praise and encourage him and lay the groundwork for him so that he may proceed without failure in whatever he does. This is in order to develop in him a strong will. If the lord is hot-blooded and short-tempered, train him to yield to your wisdom, make him constantly think to himself,

'If *he* heard of this would *he* approve?' To administer such strict training is an act of great loyalty. When there are no such retainers in the immediate surroundings, it will seem to him that the entire household flatters and fawns on him, and he will become arrogant. No matter how good the daimyo's plans for government administration, everything may be ruined by overweaning pride. All the same, very few people realize this. People like Kyūma Sagara (who served under Mitsushige) and Kichiemon Harada (who served under Katsushige, Mitsushige, and Yoshishige) paid close attention to this problem, and the young lords they served always felt their presence strongly. It is said that Yoshishige went to Kichiemon Harada even when he was ill and after his retirement. This is a desirable occurrence. It is because one believes it is difficult to fill such a role that it in fact becomes impossible. I know from personal experience that if one puts forth strenuous and unremitting effort for ten years one can become an outstanding retainer. Since it is a question of becoming an irreplaceable asset to the domain, anyone who does not try is faint-hearted and weak-spirited indeed.

The best model is Nobutaka Itagaki (retainer of Shingen Takeda). He is a person of the ilk of Takatomo Akimoto (elder statesman of the *bakufu*). Of course, if a retainer is out of favour with his lord, he will lose the opportunity to demonstrate his loyalty fully. This is an important problem, one of which few people are aware. What one must do is to train one's lord so that little by little he gains wisdom.

One Resolution After Another Add up to a Lifetime

In the last analysis, the only thing that matters is the resolution of the moment. A samurai makes one resolution after another, until they add up to his whole life. Once he realizes this, he need never feel impatient, he need seek nothing beyond the moment. He merely lives his life concentrating on his resolution. However, people tend to forget this, and to imagine that something else of importance exists. Very few realize the truth. Learning to follow one's resolution without error cannot be accomplished before the passage of many years. But after one has reached the stage of enlightenment, even if one does not consciously think about it, one's resolution will never change. If one perfects a single resolution, one will be seldom confused. This is loyalty to one's beliefs.

Nostalgia for the Past May Be Counterproductive

The climate of an age is unalterable. That conditions are worsening steadily is proof that we have entered the last stage of the Law. However, the season cannot always be spring or summer, nor can we have daylight forever. Therefore, it is useless to try to make the present age like the good old days a hundred years ago. What is important is to make each era as good as it can be according to its nature. The error of people who are always nostalgic for the old ways lies in their failure to grasp this point. On the other hand, people who value only what is up to date and detest anything old-fashioned are superficial.

Any Kind of Training Requires Both Confidence and Self-Reflection

Young men must be trained in military valour so that each has the confidence that he is the best and bravest warrior in all Japan. On the other hand, a young samurai must evaluate his discipline daily, and he must quickly discard any shortcoming he finds. Unless one divides up the subject of samurai valour in this way, one will never get anywhere.

Never Miss an Opportunity

Apparently, Kenshin Uesugi once remarked, 'I know of no trick to ensure victory. The only wisdom I have is that one must jump at every chance, never letting an opportunity slip by.' This is an interesting comment.

Abstinence in Illness

It is unwise to begin taking care of oneself only *after* having fallen ill. And it is extremely difficult to cure an illness after one has succumbed to it. Considered in the light of the Buddhist law of cause and effect, it is perfectly natural that one who does not take proper care of himself should fall ill, though it seems that even doctors do not recognize the necessity of eradicating illness before it takes hold. This is something I know for certain through direct experience. The best method of preventing illness consists of controlling one's appetite for food, drink, and sex, and to burn moxa at every spare moment. Since I was born when my parents were already of an advanced age, I was thought to have too little water in my body. At my birth the doctor's prognosis was that I would not live past twenty, so thinking that to die before I had got some enjoyment out of life and fulfilled my duties as a samurai in service would be a great pity, I made up my mind to surprise everyone and live a long life. After abstaining from sexual intercourse for seven years, I was no longer prone to illness and thus have lived on to this day. In all that time I have never once taken medicine. And whenever I was prey to slight illness, I fought it off through sheer force of will. People nowadays blame everything on their having a congenitally weak constitution, and they all die young because of over-indulgence in sex. How foolish. There is something I would like to make quite clear to doctors, and that is simply that if their patients nowadays were made to abstain for half a year, one year, or two years at the most, their maladies would cure themselves. The modern generation is mostly lily-livered and weak-willed. How can they object to being called loose and slovenly if they cannot control their appetites?

The Supreme Resolution to Die a Fanatic's Death

A samurai must take great pride in his military valour; he must have the supreme resolution to die a fanatic's death. He must do his utmost to discipline himself so that his daily thoughts, words, and deeds are all clean and pure. As for the proper way to serve the daimyo, one should consult with someone reliable, and in especially important matters with someone who is not directly involved. Throughout one's career one thinks of nothing but how to be of use to others, and it is a good idea not to know what it is not one's business to know.

When the Water Rises, So Does the Boat

There is a saying to the effect that 'when the water rises, so does the boat'. In other words, faced with hardship, human abilities increase. It is true of people of virtue and ability that the more difficulties they have to overcome, the more earnestly they cultivate their special talents. To be chagrined by hardship is a great error indeed.

What a Futile Existence

I thought about it along the way, and it occurred to me that human beings are extraordinarily cleverly devised puppets. Though they are not dangling from strings, they can walk, jump, even speak – how skilfully they are made. But all the same, before the next Bon Festival they may die and come back to visit us as spirits. What a futile existence! People always seem to forget this.

Concentrate on the Moment

This is something which Master Jōchō told his son-in-law Gonnojō: 'Now is the time, and the time is now.' We tend to think of everyday existence as different from the hour of crisis, and so when the time comes to act we are not ready;

summoned into the presence of the daimyo or sent out on a mission, we are apt to be at a loss for words. This goes to show that in our minds we separate 'the time' and 'now'. Comprehending what is meant by 'the time is now', means practising one's lines in a corner of one's room in preparation for such an occasion. Even if one is never summoned into the presence of the daimyo as long as one lives, after all a samurai must be prepared to speak out articulately before the daimyo or his elder statesmen, in public, or with the shogun himself.

This is the way to approach everything one does. It is true of practising the military arts as well as performing one's civic duties.

Do Not Encourage Weakness in Times of Distress

If a person who has met with misfortune is comforted by a half-hearted consolation such as 'I am so sorry to hear of it,' his distress and confusion will only increase to unreasonable proportions. The way to handle such a situation is to act as though nothing had happened, to try to take his mind off his troubles, remarking that things have in fact turned out for the better in some respects. In the process, the person concerned will eventually come to understand. In this uncertain world, there is no need to take each sorrow deeply to heart.

A Man's Appearance

One should always be equipped with rouge and powder. Sometimes it may happen when waking up with a hangover that one's colour is bad. At such times, one should take out one's rouge and apply it.

The Proper Way to Settle an Issue

Whenever there is to be a consultation, first talk with each person involved and then assemble the people whose opinion you need to hear, and make your decision. Otherwise, there will inevitably be people who resent your decision. Also when there is an important conference you should secretly ask the advice of people who are not directly involved. Since they have no personal interest at stake, often they understand the proper solution. If you consult people involved in the issue, they are apt to advise you in a way that will benefit them. The point is that such advice is not very useful.

Defy the Gods If They Block Your Path

If the gods are the sort to ignore my prayers simply because I have been defiled by blood, I am convinced there is nothing I can do about it, so I go ahead with my worship regardless of pollution. Although they say the gods dislike contamination, I have my own opinion on the subject. I never neglect my daily worship. Even when I get spattered with blood on the battlefield, or stumble over corpses underfoot as I fight, I believe in the effectiveness of praying to the gods for military success and long life.

Human Life Lasts But an Instant

Human life lasts but an instant. One should spend it doing what one pleases. In this world fleeting as a dream, to live in misery doing only what one dislikes is foolishness. Since this may prove harmful if misinterpreted, it is a trade secret I have decided not to pass on to young people. I like to sleep. In response to conditions in the present world, I think I shall stay at home and sleep.

Know Your Abilities and Your Limitations

Often a man of certain perceptivity is quite aware of how considerable a man he is, and he gets more and more arrogant. However, it is truly difficult to know your own strengths and weaknesses both. This statement was made by the Zen master Kaion.

Dignity

One may measure the stature of a person's dignity on the basis of external impression. There is dignity in assiduity and effort. There is dignity in serenity. There is dignity in closeness of mouth. There is dignity in observing proper etiquette. There is dignity in behaving always with propriety. There is great dignity too in clenched teeth and flashing eyes. All these qualities are externally visible. The most important thing is to concentrate on them at all times and to be totally sincere in displaying them.

Never Make Fun of a Neophyte

What follows was said by Kazuma Nakano: 'It is shabby and in poor taste to use old utensils for the tea ceremony; new ones are better.' So some people may say. On the other hand some believe that one uses old utensils because they are original artifacts. Both attitudes are mistaken. Old utensils were used by people of humble station, it is true, but their very age gives them quality, and so the old utensils have found their way into the hands of exalted personages. It is because their owners value their quality. The same thing may be said of samurai in service: A man who makes a name for himself and reaches high status though of humble origins certainly is endowed with his own quality and virtues. And yet people are extremely apt to find it disagreeable to work alongside a man of suspicious lineage, or to refuse to regard as a superior officer one who has been a mere foot soldier until now. Basically, a man who has climbed up from the rank and file has been able to do so because he has more ability and merit than those who were in an exalted position from the outset – and therefore we must accord them even more respect.

It Is Advisable To Seem Aloof from Superiors

One must seem to remain aloof from the lord of a *han*, the

elder statesmen, and senior councillors in order to achieve anything important. If one is constantly following around one's superiors and hanging on their every word, it is difficult to get things done. One should bear this in mind.

Silence Is Golden

It is wrong to speak ill of others. It is equally unbecoming to give them praise. A samurai should know his own stature, pursue his discipline with diligence, and say as little as possible.

Keep Cool

A man endowed with virtue has at core a kind of calm or ease so that he never gives the impression of being busy. It is lesser men who have no peacefulness in their character, who compete for fame and go around knocking each other down.

If You Must Fail, Fail Splendidly

In a debate or dispute of some sort, sometimes by losing quickly one loses splendidly. The same phenomenon may be seen in *sumō* wrestling. If in absolute determination to win one resorts to cheating, one is worse than a loser. One is both dirty and a loser at the same time.

Throw Yourself into Your Job with Abandon

According to my son-in-law Gonnojō, young men these days are becoming effeminate. This is an age in which people of pleasant disposition, cheerful people, people who do not cause ill feelings, gentle people, are thought to be virtuous, so that everything has become passive and strong resolution is no longer valued. If a samurai thinks only of self-preservation, he will shrink in spirit. Take you, for instance. You are probably thinking it was inexcusable to allow yourself to be adopted into another family, thereby negating not what you yourself have earned through your own merit, but what your parents obtained through hard effort: That is the conventional attitude. I disagree. While I was in service I never gave a thought to the question of merit. Since one's stipend belongs not to oneself but to one's lord, there is no reason to value it highly or part with it reluctantly. To become a ronin, or to commit ritual suicide, is in fact the final destination of the samurai in service. However, it is a shame to destroy one's family honour for an unbecoming reason. For example, one must not neglect one's duty, be carried away by selfish desires, inflict pain on others. To fail for any other reason is rather desirable than otherwise. Once you fully realize this, you will be able to make full use of your abilities and function with great energy and vigour.

Never Drop in Uninvited

Whenever you pay a call, it is advisable to check with the other party in advance. You never know what problems there may be on the other end, and if you happen to arrive at an inconvenient time, the visit will be ruined. Of course, if you happen to visit when there are other people there, you will not be able to speak freely. In particular, many slips of the tongue and errors in judgement are apt to occur at gatherings to console a man on his misfortune or bereavement.

On the other hand, no matter what trouble or confusion there may be in your home, you must never refuse to see anyone who comes to call.

A Blade That Remains in the Scabbard Rusts

Someone once said, 'There are two kinds of pride, inner and outer. A samurai who does not have both inward and outward pride is of no use.' Pride may be compared to the blade of a sword, which must be sharpened and then replaced in its scabbard. From time to time it is drawn and raised to the level of one's eyebrows, wiped clean, and then replaced in its scabbard. If a samurai's sword is always drawn and he is constantly brandishing the naked blade, people will find him unapproachable, and he will have no friends. If, on the other hand, the sword is never drawn, it will rust, the blade will become dull, and people will make light of him.

Take Things as They Come

Everyone occasionally fails at something important because he has been impatient. If one thinks there is still plenty of time, one's wishes are apt to be fulfilled more quickly. Let us simply say one's time will come. Think for a moment what things will be like fifteen years from now. Everything probably will have changed. People have written all sorts of predictions for the future, but these do not seem to predict anything strikingly different from today. Of the valuable people in service now, in ten years probably not a single one will survive. Probably only about half even of today's young people will still be alive. The world is gradually worsening; and when the silver is gone, copper becomes the treasure. With the passage of time, human abilities decrease, and so if one really pulls oneself together and makes an effort, in fifteen years' time one will become a valuable samurai. And yet, since fifteen years go by as quickly as a dream, if only you take good care of your health, eventually you will fulfil your greatest desire and serve your daimyo well. In an age of great men, it is difficult to make a name for oneself. When the world at large is going to seed, it is relatively easy to excel.

Do Not Dismiss as the Garrulity of Old Age the Wisdom of Years

One should listen with gratitude and reverence to the words of a man of many years of experience, even if he is saying something one already knows. It sometimes happens that after hearing the same thing ten or twenty times, one suddenly feels a deep, intuitive understanding. Such a revelation holds more than the usual meaning.

One tends to look down on old people and not to take their prattle seriously, but one ought to realize that after all they have had the benefit of much experience.

Never Fail Half-way

Even a failure is of no use unless a man fails thoroughly and utterly, and knows the greatest possible hardship. A man who is reliable but inflexible is not much use either.

The Priests Saigyō and Kenkō Were Cowards

As I put it in my *Foolish Reflections* (a manual of proper samurai behaviour written for his son-in-law Gonnojō), the ultimate in samurai duty is to express one's opinions as an elder statesman of the domain, an adviser to the daimyo. If one simply realized this, it would not matter what else one did or thought, but the fact of the matter is, no one does realize it. Few indeed are those whose understanding has reached such a point. Some, craving for personal advancement, fawn and flatter to better their position, but such people have smaller ambitions than to aspire to be elder statesmen. Some a little cleverer than these see nothing to gain by becoming good samurai and instead spend all their time enjoying the *Essays in Idleness* or the poetry of Saigyō. In my opinion, however, Kenkō and Saigyō are simply ineffectual cowards, nothing more. It is because they were unable to perform the duties of a samurai that they put on airs as scholar-priests in retirement from the secular world. Today, too, I suppose it is all right for priests and old people to read that sort of literature, but he who would be a samurai in the midst of his struggle for advancement in the world must serve his master faithfully and well though he plunge into Hell itself.

Hagakure: Book Three

True victory means defeating one's allies. Winning over one's allies means to achieve victory over oneself – to vanquish the body with the spirit.

Never Let Yourself Be Carried Away

I have heard that Lord Naoshige once said, 'At the time all may be friendly and jolly, and one may be enjoying oneself immensely, but afterwards there are always things one regrets having said or done.'

Sometimes It Is Wise To Overlook the Failings of Underlings

Once when Lord Katsushige was hunting at a place called Shiroishi, he shot a huge wild boar. Everyone gathered round saying what an unusually large one he had shot, when all of a sudden the boar got up and ran away. The people who had come to look were astonished and began to panic and flee. At this point, Matabei Nabeshima shot after the boar like lightning and caught it, but Lord Katsushige covered his face with his sleeve, exclaiming, 'The air is full of dust.' He evidently did this in order not to see everyone in such wild confusion.

Four Kinds of 'Salarymen'

A man called Hyōgo Naritomi once made the following remark: 'True victory means defeating one's allies. Winning over one's allies means to achieve victory over oneself – to vanquish the body with the spirit.' A samurai must daily cultivate body and spirit so that among tens of thousands of allies not one can touch him; otherwise he will certainly not be able to defeat the enemy.

Take Menial Tasks Most Seriously of All

Oribe Ikuno [elder statesman during the time of Mitsushige]

made the following statement: 'Once when Master Jōchō was young he was drinking a nightcap in the castle when Shōgen Nakano, a relative of his, said, "Tell me in your own words your understanding of samurai service." And Jōchō answered, "Since we are such close friends I will tell you freely what I think. I am totally ignorant, but it seems to me that when one has an interesting and demanding job, anyone at all may perform valid service, but given an uninteresting or demeaning task, one is apt to become depressed. This will not do – it is a waste. More than anything else a samurai's sense of duty means that even if asked to draw water and cook rice for an equal with a better job, he will not take it amiss but will perform even such a menial task with great energy and devotion. You are still young and rather precocious, and I hope you will take full notice of what I am saying." '

Sharp Wits May Lead to Arrogance

The following concerns the promotion of Ichiemon Kunō. Since Ichiemon had proved himself an exceptionally good samurai, Katsushige had been intending for quite a while to have him promoted. But because Katsushige's brother-in-law Mondo (Shigezato Nabeshima) and Ichiemon were not on friendly terms, he had hesitated to follow through with his wish. However, hearing that Katsushige was going to pay a call on Ichiemon, Mondo said to Katsushige, 'Ichiemon is a worthy retainer. Why do you not take this opportunity to promote him?' Katsushige seemed delighted and immediately summoned Ichiemon and officially promoted him, adding, 'I am relieved that Mondo seems to have changed his mind about you. You had better go and thank him.' Overjoyed, Ichiemon promptly headed for Mondo's mansion, where he thanked him for intervening on his behalf, and reverently expressed his sincere gratitude to Ichiemon in addition for having given three hundred blankets to Katsushige on the occasion of his visit to Ichiemon. When the servant who received him passed on his words to Mondo, Mondo came out to see him and said, 'I recommended that you be promoted because you are a diligent and faithful retainer. And since the daimyo was making a journey, I lent him the blankets. However, these are different matters entirely. I have no recollection of having settled our differences. Please leave this house at once and do not darken my doorway again. The blankets must be returned.' And he immediately sent someone after the blankets. Later, when Mondo was on his deathbed he summoned Ichiemon and told him, 'To tell the truth, you are an extremely sharp-witted fellow, but you are supremely self-confident, and it seemed to me you were arrogant. That is why all my life I have quarrelled with you and tried to hold you back. After I die there will be no one to bear down on you, so please at least try to be a little more humble.' They say Ichiemon was moved to tears.

How To Avoid Nervousness

When going on an important mission, before you leave put spittle on your earlobes, breathe deeply, and knock down and break something at hand. This is a secret method. Also, when you have a rush of blood to the head, if you put spittle on your earlobes you will feel better immediately.

How To Argue in a Debate

When arguing in a court of law, it is advisable to say, 'When I have considered the problem fully, I will give you my formal answer.' Even after having given a cursory answer, it is best to add, 'Let me think about this further,' thereby leaving room for a retraction if one turns out to be mistaken. Then one should consult freely with this person and that, without regard to wisdom or status. A wise man always gives you unanticipated wisdom, and if you discuss the matter with uneducated persons as well, eventually it will become public talk, which will help your cause in the end. Also, if you speak about the matter to your servants as well, explaining, 'The opponents are claiming this and that, and I am thinking of using these arguments,' taking every opportunity to rehearse your story, when the actual time comes you will be able to argue skilfully and smoothly, and you will sound absolutely reasonable. However, if you argue cold, on the basis of your own opinions, it is extremely easy to lose even if you are in the right. In any case, it is desirable to consult with others in all matters. When there is no one of wisdom or education at hand, your wife and children will do – they have their own kind of wisdom, after all. Josui Mura says too that in such a situation one needs the wisdom of age. When there are points to be made, it is a good idea to make them at once. Later on they may sound lame or like an apology. Also, at intervals you should hammer in your points, like a chicken spurring the ground. In making the opponents understand your arguments, you will do them a service by teaching them various things, and your victory will be even more splendid. This is the reasonable method of arguing.

It Is Your Disadvantage to Seem a Man of Ability

No matter how splendid a feat he may perform, a samurai who seems wise and capable at first glance will be taken for granted. When his performance is the same as his contemporaries, people will find him lacking. On the other hand, when a person who seems relaxed and easygoing does something only very slightly out of the ordinary, he will be lavishly praised.

Silence Is Best

The best conduct with regard to speaking is to remain silent. At least if you think you can manage without speaking, do not speak. What must be said should be said as succinctly, logically, and clearly as possible. A surprising number of people make fools of themselves by talking without thinking, and are looked down upon.

Start the Day by Dying

Absolute loyalty to the death must be worked at every day. One begins each day in quiet meditation, imagining one's final hour and various ways of dying – by bow and arrow, gun, spear, cut down by the sword, swallowed up by the sea, jumping into a fire, being struck by lightning, crushed in an earthquake, falling off a cliff, death from illness, sudden death – and begins the day by dying. As an old man put it, 'When you leave your own eaves, you enter the realm of the dead; leaving your gate, you meet the enemy.' This is advocating not prudence but resolution to die.

A Prerequisite for True Success

When one rises quickly in the world and one's salary is high, many people become enemies, and one's early success becomes meaningless in the long run. When, on the other hand, one is slow in making a name for oneself, many people are on one's side and one may count on still more fortune for the future. In the last analysis, it matters little whether success comes early or late; one need not worry as long as the method is acceptable to everyone. Good fortune attained with the encouragement of all is indeed genuine good fortune.

In a Major Undertaking, Minor Failures May Be Overlooked

When undertaking a great feat, do not worry about minor failures. If a samurai is absolutely loyal in his devotion to his lord, if he is brave and generous on the whole, it is no serious matter if he is selfish or mischievous once in a while.

In fact, it is rather ugly for everything always to be in perfect order – because one is apt to lose sight of the essentials. A man who accomplishes great feats must have his faults. What matters a tiny error on the part of a man of great honour and integrity?

There Is Nothing Difficult About Governing the Country and the World in Peace and Prosperity

One is apt to think that righteous government of the country and the world is an extremely difficult task, one to which most people are unequal. But if the truth be known, the elders in critical positions of authority in the central government and the councillors and elder statesmen in our own domain perform jobs that involve no special skill or wisdom outside of what I have been talking about to you in my grass hut. In fact, one may run the country brilliantly in accordance with the principles I have taught you.

In the final analysis, there is something about these people that makes me vaguely uneasy. This is because, ignorant of the traditions of our domain, failing to distinguish right from wrong, they depend on the wisdom and abilities they were born with. They have become over-confident and selfish, because everyone fears their authority, fawns on them, prostrating himself at their feet, saying, 'Yes sir, no sir, absolutely, sir, I agree with you.'